COMMISSIONER in EXILE

Author: Henry O'Donnell

Prologue and Acknowledgement by:
'Shaan' Shahrukh Dhanji

COMMISSIONER IN EXILE

PUBLISHED BY:
ZIDANE PRESS
Unit 3 Olympia Trading Estate
Coburg Road, Wood Green
London N22 6TZ

A CIP catalogue of this book is available at the British Library

ISBN: 978-0-9562678-4-9

Distributed by:
Turrnaround Publisher Services Ltd.
Unit 3 Olympia Trading Estate
Coburg Road, Wood Green
London N22 6TZ
Phone: +44(0) 20 8829 3019

TABLE OF CONTENT

PROLOGUE

"I pledge allegiance to the Flag of the United States of America, and to the Republic for which it stands, one Nation under God, indivisible, with liberty and justice for all."

By consent of the Publisher and Author, I Shahrukh Dhanji am provided the privilege of writing this prologue.

The matter of most important consideration in my struggle and journey remains the Defense and Preservation of Democracy which requires untiring and relentless vigilance. In the travails of life over the past few years I have found resolve and been nourished by conviction in God, the Love for my children and allegiance to the Constitution of the United States of America and that of my home state of Florida. The Constitution is and remains the only national legal document that I in my life have sworn to protect and defend from enemies foreign and domestic. The enemy here, that I am concerned with, is within the state.

My convictions remain steadfast, untarnished and embedded as an integral weave of my conscience. This journey has been challenging, at times quite dire, certainly emotionally and financially – and more so as I am aware for the two most important lives in my universe, my children. That most critical and vital sacrifice of time and distance from them has only been reconciled by the unwavering belief – that which heaven has bound together no man or act of man can sever. But this struggle and this fight are compelled for the need to protect and preserve a society that my and our children our entitled to, a society firmly predicated on democratic ideals that far too many lives have already been sacrificed for the posterity of generations, including ours. The current circumstances that have been the seeds of my struggle are in fact the fracture in the fundamental roots of Democratic principles orchestrated by a few "powerful political people" – in the 'land of the free and the home of the brave'. It could not in my conscience remain or go unchallenged. Evil prevails simply when Good remains silent.

I affirm and declare that the charges filed against me are in a word - laughable. There is no evidence of probative value to give an iota of credence to them – hence the independent review under European Union law that has and continues to provide me protection from open charges in the state of Florida (USA). This is a first ever for an American to be provided protection from the United States by an ally of the United States. A surrender by me under trumped up charges, which were violations of the law was not in any respect ever going to be acceptable. Certainly not in all political conscience. Very simply I would ultimately prevail against the charges filed but in doing so there would be no follow-up investigation to asses and conclude what triggered it in the first place – who had the motive, opportunity and means to commit an act that is nothing short of an assassination of the democratic electoral process.

Corruption is and remains as an internal cancer to every society it is in – arguably it is an act of internal terror. If appeased it flourishes. It is an infliction by those in public trust that violate the very sanctity of their office and position. The result in nothing less than the long lasting effect of tearing at the fabric of society they are officiated to protect and a community to serve.

The battlefields of democracy are many – often not as far as we tend to conceive.

[State Attorney Michael Satz] "Satz isn't just close to the corrupt machine that runs Broward County, he is part of it." - Bob Norman, reporting journalist.

Chapter 1. *In Defense of Law*

'When all that is rational fails, whatever remains no matter how improbable must be the truth'

In the middle of Vilnius in a darkened flat an American exile sat staring out of the window, he was thinking mainly of his two children whom he had not seen for almost 4 and half years.

An old phone in the corner of the room started ringing slowly and persistently.

He walked over, picked it up and answered 'Yes, Shaan Dhanji speaking, how can I help"

After listening intently for some time to the caller he held the phone in one hand and punched the air with his free hand, "Yes, yes, yes", he yelled as though he had just won the lottery. He sank to his knees, thanked the caller for the twentieth time and replaced the phone. Then he knelt as though in prayer, where he remained for a long time, prostrated before his God, in awe and disbelief.

His cry of vindication, was also a cry of freedom from a man in self-imposed exile, on the run from trumped-up and politically motivated criminal charges brought up against him in the state of Florida, USA. That call was to tell him that he was being given protection by Lithuania, specifically under the laws of the European Union. The date was May 21st 2013 and the reason for the protection was that his rights had been judged to have been violated by officials in the state of Florida under the cover and color of law. This was a landmark decision, and an unexpected one.

This is a true and worrying story of one Shahrukh Dhanji called Shaan by many friends and colleagues, who was once a respected Commissioner in Florida. How he went from such a position to being on the run that eventually brought him to Vilnius, the old and beautiful capital of Lithuania, is a long and complicated tale, which needs to be told.

No one expects to find themselves living in Vilnius, except Lithuanians, and an American who'd had an exemplary service in the American Navy and public service particularly hadn't planned to be there. Fate plays strange tricks on people however and as the song goes 'There but for fortune go you or I". That is the moral of this tale and why it is so important to understand the ways in which injustice can be served up just as easily as justice. Shaan Dhanji went from being an admired public servant to losing his home, his wife, his business and his reputation, and this was all through holding on to his convictions of right and wrong and his principles and an oath he had taken that he would not let go off – “I will support and defend the Constitution of the United States against all enemies, foreign and domestic, that I will bear true faith and allegiance to the same”.

Like Joseph K in Kafka’s immortal tale, he woke up one morning and found himself under attack and potential arrest through the misuse of a criminal justice system, for things that weren’t clear and which couldn’t be stated. The only word that does justice to these things is the term “Kafka-esque”. This is where charges are laid against people, but the evidence isn’t given, or is simply conveniently tainted or fabricated. Where we have seen in recent times ‘secret courts’ and ‘national security’ come into play, and where you must be guilty because you’ve been charged few things are what they seem. When you enter into politics in a state like Florida you have to watch your back, there are many vested interests in places where corruption lingers, as Shaan Dhanji was going to find out.

So who is Shaan Dhanji? And why was he hunkered down in a small flat in Vilnius waiting for a phone call from Viktor Ostrovnoj, the Chief of the Asylum Section of the Republic of Lithuania? Why was he applying for protection from the USA, and why was this highly unusual form of protection being granted for the first time ever by a small state who might well feel they could be bullied by the USA?

Almost a year and a half earlier Shaan had presented himself to the Law Enforcement Section of Lithuania's Migration Department asking for protection, for a kind of asylum. Why was he doing this? It was simple he did not believe in a surrender (a Navy man does not know surrender knowing what is right– and he had been trained by the best). He made it very clear to the Lithuanian's that what he was doing was presenting himself to an ally of the United States and asking them to look into a matter which was cancerous, it was a matter of serious "corruption" that was parasitic in his homeland, specifically within the state of Florida. He was not going to surrender to the made-up charges in Florida, to disappear into the carceral system. He wanted an independent and credible legal review from a justice system of comparable standing to that of the United States and one that is also internationally recognized. Shaan therefore asked for the appropriate legal process to be enacted under European Union laws as administered by Lithuania. The highly unusual nature of his request brought him immediately in front of the somewhat puzzled Chief of the Immigration and Border Police for the Vilnius District, Gintaras Baguzis. He was a man in his early 40s with peering eyes that gazed over Shaan in sheer astonishment. He was simply not expecting to see an American ever in his office asking for what Shaan was asking for, Personal Protection on Human Rights and Political grounds and no less than a review of the corruption matter in Florida by a friend of the United States –

Lithuania. Chief Baguzis was initially incredulous and then intrigued. His tidy office was decorated in the accustomed style of executive law enforcement offices all over the world, with regalia and memorabilia presented from other law enforcement agencies and awards impressively framed along the walls. Lithuania, of course is smaller than many states in America and having been dominated by Russia for so long, was aware of the power of other, larger countries.

On top it all these considerations Shaan only had a copy of his now expired US passport. The really easy call for Chief Baguzis and his agency would have been to simply turn down Shaan's request and to throw him out. The law provides that any person asking for asylum, refugee status or any other type of Protection coming from a "safe country" should be returned to that country unless there is compelling evidence in order to commence an investigation. The USA was clearly the international benchmark of standards for a "safe-country". America is after all the flag bearer and global leader of defending freedoms and human rights, historically exporting democracy and ensuring that the rule of law is a paramount principle. In Shaan's particular case the law however had taken a back seat to a few powerful political people, a situation that put Lithuania in a difficult position. The next 48 hours for Shaan were spent on the rack, but the answer did not come. The following day seemed to last an eternity, the hours ticking by like water dripping from a tap. All the other possibilities and requests back in his homeland that he and his friends had attempted over the course of time had not had any positive result. It was Lithuania or bust.

Shaan Dhanji had served in the American Navy, with distinction, had been an upstanding citizen, had a Doctorate in Law, and eventually was asked to become a Commissioner for Human and Civil Rights in 2005. The irony of this job is made all the more obvious when in 2009 trumped up charges were laid against him, after he had entered the race to become Sheriff in Broward County, Florida. This is a constitutional position that carries a lot of authority, and includes control of law enforcement, as well as many other areas of public work. Now he was at the mercy of the Lithuanian administration.

When you have a powerful political position like Sherriff, a position that carries a budget in access of 700 Million USD, those in an existing circle of power with things to hide don't take kindly to someone running who could expose them. These are people who have exerted for a long time control of the levers of power in Broward County and the State of Florida.

When Shaan was serving as Commissioner for the state of Florida the condition of political corruption in his home county of Broward was exemplified by the then Sheriff of Broward County, Ken Jenne a former state senator, a near lifelong politician who had just been indicted and convicted under Federal Bribery charges. This man was part of the Old Boys bunch. The same bunch of Old Boys that Mike Satz the very long serving State Attorney is a part off. This man has now been in office 40 years and counting – since Gerald Ford was President of the United States. These people wanted to make sure that their hold and influence over key official positions was retained. This meant you did not let players onto the political field of influence and control who were outsiders to this circle of the few power hungry but well positioned politicians. Shaan was the outsider.

America is a democracy and anyone can stand for any position they like, so Shaan Dhanji did just that, and received many endorsements from many people for his campaign. Perhaps he made the mistake of announcing that if his campaign was successful he was going to seriously crackdown on corruption. People in positions of power, particularly if they have been there for a long time, do not like light been thrown on their activities, and they particularly do not like people who try to take over their jobs and clean things up. Old boy networks seem to exist everywhere, and, like the Mafia, are a means of controlling power in the interests of that network. These kinds of networks operate in secret and the one thing that threatens them are citizens who are prepared to throw light on that secrecy.

This is very probably why Shaan Dhanji went from being an upstanding citizen running for Sherriff to being the first American in history to be provided protection from open criminal charges in the United States by a NATO and EU ally of the United States. These charges in the state of Florida stemmed from a corrupt investigation that violated the basic fundamentals of basic Human Rights. It may seem somewhat extreme to say so but in America there have been so many murders of people standing up for human rights and freedom, from Martin Luther King to John and Bobby Kennedy, that clearly the basic tenets of the idea of freedom before the law are often tested. Shaan Dhanji was one of a long line of people who have stood against corruption and paid the price. Is it a price worth paying? That is one of the truly difficult questions to answer.

Shaan S, Dhanji, the new resident of Vilnius, Lithuania was born into an upright, large family in Bombay (now called Mumbai) he was brought up with those traditional family values of loyalty, service and respect for family and community, values that are universal and particularly respected in America. Public service to the community was in the lifeblood of his parents and grandparents, and so he was to continue that tradition.

Shaan left India for the USA when he was eight, hardly old enough to know much but knowing that this was the ultimate destination- the land of the free. Born in

Bombay he ended up in the splendidly named Coconut Creek, Florida - a fully-fledged, American educated, American citizen. His early years in America were fairly ordinary, possibly even uneventful, doing well at school at West Hollywood Private School and graduating at 18 as valedictorian, basically the kid with the best results in the year. While in high school he found a job at 17 as a courier at a well-respected law firm of Becker, Poliakoff and Strietfeld. (The latter Strietfeld later became a Judge, whom Shaan would recommend for the appellate bench in Florida years later). Once again Shaan demonstrated those principles of hard-work and achievement that are meant to define the American dream, starting at the bottom and eventually working his way through law-school, and on to a distinguished career. This was the classic path of the immigrant, work hard, study, get involved in the community and get on through sheer hard work and ability. Shaan joined the Navy reserves and for eight years served with merit in many roles. He had a Top Secret security clearance for most of those years, was a qualified Sharpshooter, conducted ship boardings, instructed small craft inland channel navigation and left with an honourable discharge. His commanding officer, one Commander Eugene Ford, Jr., recommended Shaan to apply for a commission in the officer ranks and he wrote "He has unlimited potential and capacity for future important assignments and increased responsibility. He is thorough in his assignments and exhibits a sound decision making process. ... I would be happy to serve with him as an officer and give him my highest recommendation" This is not the profile of a trouble-maker or a political deviant, it is the record of a good citizen. Machiavelli once famously pointed out that one of the ways in which to stay in power was to have two faces, one that promised friendly things and one that was vicious like a Lion. Shaan Dhanji was to discover the way in which this is still very true, and how.

The ways in which Government officials swear to uphold the law, and proper behavior, are fairly well known, even Richard Nixon was always claiming to be an upholder of the truth of his office. Maybe Mr. Dhanji was a little naïve when he followed the footsteps of others and promised obedience and fealty to the upholding of his office and of civic duty.

In Florida there is a pretty long history of malfeasance in public office, described, for example, in a case concerning a state official in the Florida Supreme Court in 2000 as being "Malfeasance, as without lawful grounds she makes every effort to deprive applicants of their rights of due process of law." (Case No NSC94751) This was what was going to happen to Mr Dhanji later.

The case against Mr. Dhanji goes to the very essence of a corrupt system where there is a complete absence of any due process. Where those in public positions set up an "investigation" to serve the interest of "powerful political people" and to protect themselves at the cost of the law and of Democratic values.

Trying to assert these rights has cost him a great deal and explains why, in the end, Lithuania granted him protection, because he is able to show the ways in which his rights, legal and human, had been illegally taken away from him. Power corrupts, and getting power in Florida, is quite a corrupting process. Simply assuming that the law operates in a clear and unbiased manner is, in reality, a rather naïve view of life in the Sunshine state.

Take this much more recent example from Watchdog Wire, Florida, November 5th, 2013. -this was a letter from a group of concerned citizens to the state office.

"We the undersigned, ask that your office immediately launch an investigation into the possibility of widespread official misconduct potentially involving fraudulent activity and malfeasance, by elected and appointed officials. While our concerns are primarily involved with SE Florida, the results of such an investigation may affect all Floridians, with likely national ramifications."
In case anybody thinks there is exaggeration going on here is a report that has just emerged from the organization called Integrity Florida and reported in the HuffPost Miami (March 9th 2014)

(http://www.huffingtonpost.com/2012/06/07/florida-most-corrupt-in-country_n_1577571.html)

A new study by nonprofit Integrity Florida ranks the Sunshine State (Florida) as the country's most corrupt.

According to the "Corruption Risk Report: Florida Ethics Laws," 1,762 of Florida's public officials have been convicted of public corruption since 1976. From 2000 to 2010, there have been an average of 71 convictions each year -- and 107 convictions in 2000 alone, the worst year on record."

This looks like a state where corruption has been an endemic problem for a long time, and probably one where people should tread really carefully when poking into the viper's nest.

There was a famous British general who was risk averse to starting wars and he was quoted as having said 'The trouble with snakes is, if you poke 'em, they bite you". Funnily enough he was in Iraq during the 1st World War when he said this.

Shaan perhaps should have heeded these words when he launched his campaign to denounce and expose corrupt officials. However, during the earlier years his career as a public servant had been straightforward and even distinguished. He held many positions on District boards, had been involved in much community work and eventually, in 2005, was asked by Jeb Bush, Governor of Florida, to become a Commissioner for Human and Civil Rights. His work involved developing and enhancing community cohesion, legal protection of ALL and ensuring that the legal processes related to human rights were sufficient. Shaan set up the Human Relations Council of Florida in 2006 in a joint enterprise with the State of Florida, in order to further these aims. His work in these areas was summed up by a Rabbi he worked with in enhancing community cohesion, and was addressed to the Governor.

To the Governor of the state of Florida:

*What makes our relationship even more unique and should tell you something special about this man is the fact that although we come from diametrically different backgrounds and faiths, not only has it not been an impediment, but rather we've come to learn from and respect each other even more. ….. His relationship with the Broward Jewish community is exceptional. …. I, and my fellow Jewish clergymen and our respective communities know we can count on him and I know you can as well. "**Rabbi Joseph I. Korf** (Florida, USA)".*

There were many commendations of his work and his profile was steadily increasing, so much so that in May 2007 he was asked by the Chief Judge of the 17th circuit of the state of Florida to take up a position “to redeem the public trust and confidence in their judges”. This was an interesting development because it further showed that there were problems with the public perception of the legal system, and with endemic corruption in the state of Florida. Taking all this on was a pretty daunting task and entailed a serious commitment to building new politics in Florida. It was these sorts of experiences that eventually led Commissioner Dhanji to think about standing for the position of Sherriff, a position that carried a great deal of power and influence, and which was held or controlled by long serving politicians like Jenne and the still serving State Attorney Mike Satz. Satz has been in the position of State Attorney for nearly 40 years, making him the longest serving state attorney in Florida’s history. This was a man who saw himself as entitled to his position and was not very keen on people looking into the shenanigans of himself or his “friends”. Now Commissioner Dhanji in his candidacy for sheriff decided to do just that and, as they say, the rest is history.

Sitting in his little flat in Vilnius having just gained protection by Viktor Ostrovnoj, the Chief of the Asylum Section of the Republic of Lithuania, under the provisions of the European Union’s Human Rights Convention - the first American to do so, Shaan had ample time to reflect on the complicated, difficult and almost unbelievable story that had brought him from his large, comfortable house in Coconut Creek, Florida, in the bosom of his wife and children, to this strange, if hospitable, country that had itself only recently emerged from the grip of the Soviet Union. Like the Ancient Mariner he had a tale to tell, and he was going to tell it.

Shahrukh Dhanji (Shaan) with Gintaras Baguzis, Chief of Migration Police (Vilnius District)

Chapter 2. *Call to Service*

"Ask not what your country can do for you, Ask what you can do for your country."
– John F. Kennedy (Presidential inaugural speech 1961)

It was a warm, dry sunny December day in 2005, and Shaan was socializing with his friend and colleague Victor Smirnow, at a restaurant started by Victor – called the Gaucho Rodizio. Victor was another successful immigrant who had made it in America. He was a retired senior executive from General Motors who had started a Brazilian Steakhouse, the largest of its kind in Florida at the time – the Gaucho Rodizio. It was a sprawling, spacious 15000 square feet restaurant with bars, banquet and dining facilities that was located in the ocean front city of Lighthouse Point, a small city in the bustling texture of Broward County. Victor hailed originally from Kaunas, Lithuania, and had lost his father in the violent events that followed when the Soviets had invaded in 1940. Victor was then but a child and this clearly had a major effect on him; and to add to this trauma his mother had re-married, to a German officer whom she met when the Germans entered Lithuania during their invasion of the then Soviet Union. Ultimately when the Soviet Union regained the edge and drove the Germans back with

Germany losing the war, his adopted father and whole family ultimately migrated, settling in Brazil. Victor grew-up in Brazil, still holding on to his family roots and heritage in Lithuania. He graduated with degrees in engineering which brought him to work for General Motors and as a result to the United States. Ironically, years later he would be in the hierarchy of the GM lead team that brought GM into Russia. The Brazil connection was also why he ended up setting a Brazilian steak house, something that chimed well with the American food culture.

As a close friend and colleague, Victor had invited Shaan to become a partner in the restaurant Gaucho Rodizio. In 2000, Shaan had accepted the offer and became a partner in the business. They would meet regularly at the Rodizio to discuss business matters and to chew the fat. A fairly routine day in the late afternoon was changed rather dramatically when Shaan got a call from the office of then state Governor, Jeb Bush (his brother George Bush was the 43rd President of the United States at the time).

The caller asked- Is this Mr. Dhanji?"
"Yes, was the reply - Followed by – "Who is this?"

"We are calling to ask if you would be willing serve the state as a Commissioner for Human and Civil Rights?"

“Yeh, sure who is this really?” Shaan replied, convinced it was a hoax call from a friend.

The caller from the Governor’s staff then made it clear that this was a genuine call and asked if he would accept the position of Commissioner for Human and Civil Rights. This was an important position that would involve a great deal of community activity. It was a commission that also needed to raise its profile of existence in order to increase awareness to the people that it was there to serve. Shaan had not seriously anticipated any such invitation for public service at this level. After all he was a Democrat, and the Bush administration was Republican. Florida itself was a pretty staunchly Republican place as well. Only when the caller asked in a fairly formal and official tone if he was refusing the position did Shaan fully understand this was no prank call but an official invitation to serve the people of the state of Florida. It would be fair to say that he was pretty gob-smacked by this turn of events.

Under the Bush administration he was the only Commissioner in this position from the Democratic Party serving a Republican Administration (twice) -the position was one of service to community – protecting the very basis of human rights and self-determination. Since Florida is an expanding state, and its historical expansion has been mostly fueled by immigration, the role of Commissioner was going to be increasingly important in ensuring that human and civil rights were protected and understood. Florida has grown steadily over the last twenty years and could soon overtake New York in economic importance.

"Florida's growth for many years has been due primarily to migration," Stan Smith said. "Typically, 80 to 90% of growth in the state has to do with people moving in." (Stan Smith, population program director at the University of Florida's Bureau of Economic and Business Research (BEBR). This spike in immigration includes people moving from other states as well as from abroad, bringing dynamism to the state economy. Based on responses to BEBR surveys most people moving to Florida do so for job-related reasons. The state also draws retirees seeking a warmer climate. Florida is thus a massive melting pot of peoples from everywhere and the task of building a widespread understanding of civil rights was important both from the legislative point of view and from the people's point of view. This was to be Shaan Dhanji's aim and political intention.

A quick break down of the Florida economy is useful to give the background picture. In 2005 the overall state domestic gross product was $680,277, 000. The main components of the economy are -- International Trade (40% of all U.S. exports to Latin and South America pass through Florida) Tourism - with 87.3 million visitors in 2011 (a record number), Florida is the top travel destination in the world. The tourism industry has an economic impact of $67 billion on Florida's economy. The Space Industry represents $4.1 billion of the state's economy. Agriculture - Florida leads the southeast in farm income. Florida produces about 67% of the U.S. oranges and accounts for about 40% of the world's orange juice supply. Construction - This industry's strength results from the steady stream of new residents and visitors who are welcomed to Florida each year. Financial Services, health economy and software business are smaller but still significant. This is a rich state with a low tax base, one of the lowest in America, which means that state spending is also relatively limited. Being a rich state means that business can do very well, and state officials not being well paid means that they may well be open to corruption and bribery. This is partly why Florida has gained a reputation as one of the most corrupt states in America.

During the early 2000's Shaan's public service had been growing alongside his business interests, beginning with being a representative on the Mediator Qualifications Board – in the State of Florida. This era could be called the "age of innocence", when everything was taken at its face value and one assumed that everyone else was working for the good of the community. This was followed by being a representative on the Public Safety Board – Broward County, the Environmental Health Board –Broward County, and the Natural Resource Protection Board –

Broward County, and then the Mental Health Board District 10 – State of Florida. This broad range of positions gave him valuable experience and, of course, led to him building an extensive network of contacts. It was through this wide spread and successful community activity that his nomination for the role of Commissioner was to come.

It was undoubtedly through his friend Keith Roberts that the nomination likely originated. He was a long-time friend and had been Shaan's Best Man at his wedding, a fairly important role. Keith was a former US Marine who after his service in the military had joined the US Border Patrol and risen to the rank of Assistant Chief, US Border Patrol. Interestingly he had been involved in the media frenzy that surrounded the affair of the young Cuban boy Elian Gonzalez' and his custody battle and his return to Cuba for reconciliation with his father. Keith Roberts was the stereotype of a marine, being tall, lean and fit. An African-American with noticeable stature, his presence alone was commanding, especially when in uniform. In everyday demeanor he was soft spoken, and always exercised caution and prudence. Like the wisdom of Sun-Tzu going back 2,500 years he always used the "pause" not to be quick on the trigger. After retiring from the US Border Patrol he went on to do a short time with the anti-smuggling operations end with the US Department of Homeland Security. Keith and others started to re-connect with Shaan on social media networks after

Lithuania's / EU protection kicked in and Shaan's position was known.

Shaan had first met Keith at a dinner at the Riverside Hotel in Ft. Lauderdale, memorializing the death of an on duty Florida State Trooper Kimberly Ann Hurd. Trooper Hurd was killed when she was struck by a drunk driver while talking with the driver of another car she had stopped. The drunk driver who struck Trooper Hurd, a retired police officer, fled the scene but was later apprehended and convicted.

Shaan was at that time also with the Broward Sheriff's Advisory Council – Sheriff Nick Navarro had created this council in the interest of a more integrated and improved relationship between law enforcement and community. Navarro was a charismatic and flamboyant personality as a crime fighter and law enforcement executive. As Sheriff he had brought a spotlight to shine on the Broward Sheriff's Office as the inaugural department to be aired on the COPS, TV show. It was the show that brought the reality of everyday crime fighting and personal feel of law enforcement off the streets into the TV household for all to see. He made the office into a drugbuster operation cleaning up the streets and many neighborhoods. This was the Sheriff that also authorized the manufacture of look-a-like drugs in the police labs to conduct sting operations. He took his commitment to the overall safety of the community he swore to protect and serve, seriously.

Shaan was among a select 100 from the community chosen by Navarro with the rank of Major within the Advisory Council.

After that eventful first meeting with Keith the two became close friends often engaging in charitable and societal activities for the improvement and betterment of community. Their joint community activities included the Starting Place, a counseling and treatment facility for adolescents with dependency issues; also bicycle gift programs to the young from bicycles that had been found or confiscated by law enforcement agencies. Occasions such as Birthdays, social events and Thanksgiving holidays were spent together. It seems fairly clear that Keith had suggested Shaan for consideration to serve as the Commissioner, especially since, Keith too had been in service as a state Commissioner for Human Relations.

The post of commissioner was one of twelve serving critically to establish policy and direction as well as to serve as adjudicators on panels of three when hearing appeals from decisions made by commission investigators. This was a commission charged with protecting human and civil rights of all who came to live, work or vacation in the state of Florida. It was the states version of the Federal 1964 Civil Rights Act. Community harmony and issues related to Human Trafficking and Hate Crimes also became an integral aspects of the commissions function. Although the commission had been in existence for decades much of its work, importance and powers to protect classes of people in the state were not widely known or understood. Although nominated by the Governor, Shaan also had to go through confirmation of appointment by the Florida Senate. This too was a process which ended in success, and was not necessarily a foregone conclusion. He was sworn in at a ceremony at the commission office shortly after Senate confirmation in early 2006.

One of the initiatives Shaan wanted to undertake was to raise awareness of this commission and its work, which was a vital responsibility to over 50 million people who live, work or visit Florida. His thinking was fairly straightforward- you cannot serve the people you are supposed to if they don't know you exist. He shared this idea of the need for greater awareness with various close friends, and met with much agreement. After all awareness lends to increasing local community involvement, which in turn ultimately empowers individuals with knowledge of their rights. Once there is knowledge and awareness of rights there is a reduced propensity of people allowing others to take advantage or abusing other people. Like anywhere, even in the state of Florida it was of critical importance for people to know their rights under the law – what protections and services are available. No doubt this position carried an important role for the overall community and politically.

The impact of becoming the Commissioner was considerable – and was widely recognized. Judge Peter Skolnik a friend and former professor of Shaan's came up with the idea of holding a reception to commemorate the appointment and to celebrate the confirmation of the new Commissioner – Shahrukh Dhanji. After some discussion amongst friends it was agreed that this was a good way to promote the whole idea of the Commission and its work to the community at large.
Another friend Ted Sahagian, a business leader in South Florida and the former Chairperson of the Broward Sherriff's Advisory Council helped organizing the committee for the reception. Through this process others were invited to participate and join. One such person was Howard Gressman – who soon became a very close friend, supporter and business colleague. Howard was very like the persona of the older brother or uncle you could always go to and talk to about anything. He almost always had had an answer or just the right kind of conversation and time with Howard was therapeutic. Howard was a quintessential good listener – thoughtful, kind – a loyal and trusted friend, and he was always good for a vodka or a whiskey with a cigar. He was also full of compassion which he balanced with wisdom and the ability to act as warranted by situation and circumstance. They had first meet in Ted Sahagian's office as part of the organizing committee to plan the event idea formulated by Judge Skolnik. After that

meeting had concluded and all the participants had left, Shaan and Howard spent a couple hours talking in the parking lot – it was as though two lost brothers had found each other. This relationship would remain unfettered, unwavering and staunchly loyal.

Victor Smirnow graciously provided the facilities of the Rodizio for the reception. There were in the end over 500 invited guests attended, and this was clearly a fairly high profile event. The Chairs for the occasion were Sheriff Nick Navarro (retired), Lori Parrish (Property Appraiser) and Howard Foreman (Clerk of the Courts), respectively. Federal Judge Marcia Cooke agreed to serve as the Honorary Chair. She was the first African-American woman appointed to the Federal Bench in the Southern District of Florida. Shaan had first met her through Keith when she was newly appointed to serve in the US Attorney's office of the Southern District of Florida. She later left the US Attorney's office and became Inspector General for the state of Florida for JEB Bush when he was Governor. Sometime after she was nominated and confirmed onto to the Federal Bench. Judge Cooke (Marcia) for all the obvious legal and social and historical reasons took a keen interest in the purpose and mission of the Commission. Invited attendees commemorating the recent confirmation of Shaan as Commissioner included members of the South Florida judiciary, elected officials, enforcement professionals, and community and business leaders, respectively. The success of the reception was realized not only by the attendees but also by the community awareness that followed.

Interest in the commission and its work grew and there was a grass roots effort from community groups to get more involved. Approaches were made by senior citizen groups, home owners and condominium associations, programs for children and schools were being developed – with statewide impact.

One of the strategies was to undertake to partner with local community leaderships. In order to bring some structure to this process and build political capital a "Friends of the Commission" ad hoc committee was proposed. Eventually Shaan established, in December of 2006, the Human Relations Council of Florida (HRC), a not-for profit organization. In recognizing the many financial challenges that face government agencies in Florida the Not for Profit form was clearly the correct strategy. It was an autonomous yet strategically connected to the commission, by mission and objective - which made good sense. Much of the initial development of this organization was taken on by Shaan and his close associates like Howard Gressman and Cooper City Commissioner John Sims. As time went on, John's wife, Janet also got very involved contributing much of her time to organizing the various activities that the Council promoted. John was also former US Navy and had been something of a political maverick - coming in without party affiliations to get elected to a city commission. When Shaan first approached John with idea of running for Sheriff, John was the first city elected official to endorse the candidacy – stating "What do you have to loose – an election?" Little did he or Shaan now how much there was too loose.

The HRC was formed and now it needed and Executive Director to lead it and manage its daily operations. The first operational Executive Director of the HRC was Norman Price, who had been the former vice-mayor of the smallest municipality in Broward County – Pembroke Park. He had just finished his employment with the Supervisor of Elections office and was eager to start something new. Having known each other through community events, Norman suggested he would have the time to undertake activities and lead on the HRC. Shaan was pleased to have someone help and to take over the "daily push", running the organization. Unfortunately what was not known at the time was that Norman had a prescriptive drug dependency issue, something that was clearly going to become a problem. Not having known Norman on daily basis previously this was a completely unknown fact to everyone involved. Taking people on trust is, of course, a hazardous business in politics, skeletons in the cupboard is something that the media specialize in finding out! Quite soon other issues started to filter out, all of which were real problems. It turned out that

Norman had fathered a child and boasted of his success at not taking the responsibility of being a father. In fact, in time Norman's psychological issues also began to surface. He had been emotionally and psychologically devastated having seen his father commit suicide, with a revolver. More information about Norm Price started to surface this time from Ron Cacciatore. Cacciatore was a former Captain in the Broward Sheriff's Office in the time when Navarro had been the Sheriff. Cacciatore was affectionately called "the chicken" amongst friends– because of his ethnic roots and from the food dish that emanates from the Italian palate. Cacciatore had a certain charm about him, always easy going with a smile that was hard to read, one could never tell quite which side he was on except truly on his own side. He too had something of a colorful past that included a Federal indictment and an allegation of Fraud in excess of 150,000 USD. Ultimately the indictment was dismissed – but many questions had remained unanswered. After leaving the Sheriff's office his trail of employment brought him to work for Lori Parrish the County's Property Appraiser, as her Chief Investigator. Cacciatore pretty much had the low down on anyone that had been on an elected position in Broward County and that included Norm Price. So Cacciatore made it known to Shaan that Norman had a tendency to engage in prostitution, and to do so rather frequently. This type of behavior is not only ethically abhorrent, but also illegal. Prostitution is a known feeder to Human Trafficking, and associated with organized crime and drugs, not exactly the profile that the Human Relations Council was trying to establish. This type of behavior was quite abhorrent to Shaan, and to the people he was working with to bring a new kind of politics to Florida. This kind of politician was basically typical of much of the unchecked activities of "Old Boys' network and that which surrounded them that ran things in the state, and presumably thought that Shaan Dhanji and the efforts of the newly formed not-for-profit council was simply old wine in new bottles. Shaan grew incensed that these facts had not been disclosed to him earlier on. He spoke to Norman Price, and asked him to resign his position with the HRC, and to quietly slip away, describing issues of a personal nature for the separation and resignation. In fact Shaan strongly suggested to Norman that he get professional counselling and begin to work on engaging in some manner with the child he had fathered. This direct and honest approach and the delusional mind of Norman Price would come to adversely impact Shaan during his later campaign.

Sheriff Nick Navarro with Shaan's wife and son, Zayn (to whom Navarro had presented a Deputy Sheriff's Star when he was a year Old. Zayn (here 9 years of age) is seen here wearing the Star on his suit lapel pointed to by Navarro

Chapter 3. *Commissioner –In Service*

“My brother Bob doesn't want to be in government - he promised Dad he'd go straight.”
- John F. Kennedy

“The Florida in my novels is not as seedy as the real Florida. It's hard to stay ahead of the curve. Every time I write a scene that I think is the sickest thing I have ever dreamed up, it is surpassed by something that happens in real life.” - Carl Hiaasen

---

Shaan Dhanji started his service as a Commissioner in 2006 and quickly got his feet under the table. There were many things to do, getting the office up and running, defining the parameters of the job, meeting the right people and, of course, trying to reach out to the population of Florida. It was also going to be interesting to find out what the scope of the job was, and what was possible to achieve in such a large, and extremely mixed, State. It was fairly obvious from the start that it was going to be different. The sorts of civil rights questions and difficulties that the role of Commissioner was to involve very soon became apparent to no Commissioner Dhanji.

It was just another clear, sunny mid- day in Florida when Shaan got another phone call that was to have important consequences. He was on the terrace connected to his office with his partner and friend Howard Gressman. The two were in discussion on the upcoming possibility of a commercial venture. The call came from one Iqbal Lakhani. He was the secular leader for the community of the followers of the Aga Khan, who are known as Ismailis – a Muslim sect. It turned out he had just been contacted by a counterpart of his from the Sunni sect of Islam from Tampa, Florida. What Iqbal Lakhani had to tell Shaan was that his counterpart in Tampa had informed him that somebody had spray painted the word Jihadist across the lawn of a home of a Muslim family in an affluent gated community in Tampa. This kind of hate crime had a long history in the Deep South, from Klu Klux Klan cross burnings as a symbol of threat to implant fear, sometimes as a pre-signature for murder and mayhem. In Florida there had also been swastika symbols vandalizing Jewish places of work and worship. These actions were deeply intolerant, societally heinous and were fundamentally Hate Crimes. This was something the commission was engaged in combating in alliance with law enforcement agencies and local prosecutor offices.

It had become obvious post 9/11 that a new target had arisen, and that the atmosphere of cultural tolerance had worsened considerably. Previously separate groups, smaller communities who had been relatively invisible, were being lumped together and seen as an 'outsider' group. These were different groups of people that in actuality shared very little – but to bigots no social differences were recognized between the South Asian and the Middle Eastern people, nor any distinction seen in the religious and cultural differences between these different peoples. A cover-all term of abuse saw all these peoples as "Muslim's", whatever that meant. These intolerant perceptions ignored the reality that the vast majority of immigrants from these regions of the world that came to make America home were patriotic, law abiding and productively contributing members of their communities. Civil rights and human rights were once again under pressure from a vociferous minority who basically believed in the "old" America, which was conceived of as white. Interestingly Americans of South Asian descent are one of the fastest-growing ethnic groups in the U.S.A and are also one of the most successful, with high education attainments and high income. Despite this cadre of academic and professional achievements, there are still many who, post 9/11 see them all as potential terrorists.

Shaan was faced with the question of what could be done, and what could the commission do? – How would the affected homeowner and his family be protected? There was a clear fear that property damage and loss might occur and more importantly imminent physical harm or life itself within this gated community. Here was the re-appearance of a modern day cross burning – usually planted on the front lawn of the target – which is exactly what the spray painting of the word JIHADIST on the lawn of a Muslim immigrant homeowner was meant to signify. It was well known historically that leaving unchecked these sorts of hate crimes have generally lead to a growth of communal unrest or certainly something far more dangerous, leading to criminal acts of violence.

On reflection Shaan advised that the homeowner should report this attack to local law enforcement and then later to the FCHR Commission office in Tallahassee. His phone call ended with the usual pleasantries and agreement. Then a few minutes later another call from Iqbal Lakhani came through and informed Shaan that the Commission office in Tallahassee informed the complainant / victim that this was not a matter for the commission nor was Tampa an area of authority for the commission. Shaan assured Lakhani that this matter would be redressed within the hour.

President, Harry S. Truman had summed up the position about the government and civil rights pretty well in a speech to Congress in 1945 when he said:

"Every segment of our population, and every individual,

has a right to expect from his government a fair deal." (Speech to Congress 6th September 1945.)

When there is an absence of vigilance to protecting the fundamental values of democratic societies; those of life, liberty, property, and equality, then society tends to fall back into ancient ways of discrimination. 9/11 ushered in such a period when civil rights were trampled on and there was failure to challenge hate and ignorance. Bizarrely one of the first fatalities after 9/11 among South Asians was Balbir Singh Sodhi, an upstanding Sikh targeted because of his turban. On September 15, 2001, Sodhi, a Sikh-American, was murdered outside his gas station in Mesa, Arizona by Frank Roque, who said he wanted to 'kill a Muslim' in retaliation for the terrorist attacks" Sikhs, of course, are descended from Hindu's and nothing whatever to do with Muslims, a minor detail to a bigot.

The lack of action in the face of the smallest grievous acts opens a crack that can ultimately fracture the very democratic base of a society, and not challenging the anti- Muslim attacks in America was a clear case in point. Shaan called the Commission office in Tallahassee and asked to speak to the Chief Legal Counsel, one Cecil Howard and the Executive Director Derrick Daniels, respectively. When he got them on the phone he asked them 2 simple questions. (1) Had Tampa been ceded from the state of Florida? and (2) is the Commission charged with protecting all the people in the state of Florida? Both men were perplexed by these questions. Owing to the existing protocols of their office the men answered the questions, but with some clear reluctance. The first question was answered by a NO and the second by a YES. Now that the clear basis of this call had been established the conversation went further. It was also clear however that a call from the Commissioner was not expected. It transpired however that the gentlemen were not aware that the intake operator had refused and failed to take in the complaint from Tampa. This call certainly lead to a minor awakening that the Commissions vigilance was required at all times, without exception. Within a week the commission had organized a Town Hall meeting in the impacted community in Tampa. Agencies from the Federal, State and local level were represented. This kind of incident was never repeated again.

The Commission in Florida did and continues to do excellent work. Its' successes are often not acclaimed – but that is the nature of the work. Incidents like these do not happen often but there is no room for exceptions, complacency or the tolerance of abuse when individual rights are infringed, compromised or threatened. As someone said, "the price of freedom is eternal vigilance."

It was clear in Florida that the social and racial tensions ignited by 9/11 were going to present problems. Of note was an incident where ironically it was the African

American community which took exception to the building of a mosque in an area where there was also a church represented by Rev Dozier and attended predominantly by African Americans. Now unfortunately in these situations there are often people who seek to exploit such community conflagrations, and there are many who follow the fire-brands and the media are happy sell on the frenzy. Facts get hidden by the controversy or are drowned out by the drama makers, the media loves drama a thousand times more than boring facts. Attempts at resolution take cooler and hopefully more sensible heads to prevail and bring about the understanding and harmony necessary for any community to grow evolve and succeed. After weeks of high octane abuse and posturing, a local African American Bishop approached Shaan to see if alternative lines of communication could be opened in order to resolve the dispute. Shaan was, and is, a strong proponent of Conflict Prevention and Resolution – as long as lines of communication remain open there are always possibilities. Shaan approached Altaf Ali, the regional head of CAIR. (Council of American Islamic Relations). He then arranged for the two key figures to meet privately, where Shaan, being a licensed and experienced mediator, provided the facilities and professionalism to commence a discussion. At least for a time after this meeting the frenzy slowed down. Ultimately, the matter was redressed in the courts before Judge Strietfeld. The mosque building was constructed as had been previously approved by the

City of Pompano Beach. Both leaders of the respective groups later wrote to the Governor of Florida praising Shaan's efforts in bringing together the two divergent groups.

To the Governor of Florida:

"Recently, Commissioner Dhanji Assisted in resolving a very delicate and potentially explosive situation. ... Commissioner Dhanji successfully established an alternative dialogue between the affected African American and Muslim communities in Pompano Beach, Florida; establishing mutual understanding, respect and offering solutions ..."
Bishop Tommy Troutman

"Kindly accept my commendation of Commissioner Shahrukh Dhanji ... For the expert manner in which he had assisted the Muslim and African-American communities in Pompano Beach Florida. The Commissioner accomplished the desired goal of establishing respect, understanding and cooperations in a time of crisis. He is most adept at bringing people together."
Altaf Ali, Exec Dir. CAIR (Florida, USA)

Another fascinating area of work that Shaan got involved in was with the Judges in Florida, who, it is fair to say, had a bit of an image problem. One writer described the situation like this: The State of Florida is now rated near the bottom in Legal Fairness (Harris Poll), some 70% of Floridians do not trust attorney's (Florida Bar Study), the Florida Bar's own statistics state that 14% to 20% of lawyers and judges suffer impairment disorders including on-going cocaine addiction (Florida Lawyers Assistants Program), yet these legal practitioners continue, shielded by the rules and laws created by a self-serving Florida Bar. (Newswire.com)

In May of 2007 a certain Judge Charlie Greene came under attack in the media for using the term NHI. (This means in code "no humans involved" a way of referring to murders of suspected criminals or racialized suspects who are not seen as worthy of attention) The disclosure was made by the Assistant Public Defender who overheard Judge Greene use the term shortly after he had adjourned the jury for deliberation on the verdict. This was a homicide case involving African-Americans, and this kind of covert racism was seen as an endemic problem in the Southern states.

This one incident brought attention onto the rest of the judicial system and the media started to focus on the behaviour of Judges. One Judge Korda was caught smoking marijuana in a Hollywood Park. Larry Seidlin, the judge presiding over the infamous Anna Nicole Smith case was seen crying in court – arguably producing his own drama scene, and possibly auditioning for a future TV role. CNN legal analyst Jeffrey Toobin referred to him as "Judge Judy's wacky little brother." Another Judge, Robert Zack had been accused of taking gifts and loans from attorneys practicing before him. The last matter involving Judge Zack actually came to light from an attorney who was a former Judge himself – Chris Roberts. Chris Roberts was at a time the youngest Judge in the history of Florida, who had been removed from the bench when his dependency on alcohol had resulted in actions placing risk to public safety. The number of cases against judges was simply quite staggering. This can all be read in the highly entertaining work "***A Most Disorderly Court: Scandal and Reform in the Florida Judiciary.***" (Martin A. Dyckman.)

In the case where the judge used the term "NHI" it seemed that since African Americans were involved there was an allegation that the Judge was racist and therefore biased. The media had a field day, not surprisingly. Judge Peter Skolnik, who was somewhat embarrassed by this event, called Shaan and asked if he could join him in chambers. Shaan's office was just across the street from the courthouse and so he informed the Judge that he could be with him in about half an hour. Skolnik had been a long serving Judge with a deep and sincere care for the Florida community. He wanted to assess the various alternatives to address community concerns while the Judges faced attack after attack in the media. He too wanted to know if there was any substance to the matters alleged, and how things could be improved. He asked if there was anything the Commission could do.

Shaan replied by saying as a commissioner he would look into the matter if invited to do so with the appropriate authority on behalf of the Judges so requesting. Shaan wanted to help but only in an advisory role. To make recommendations as warranted. It was not otherwise his purview or that of the Commissions to engage into this matter. There were other lead organizations to deal with this matter, such as the Judicial Qualifications Committee made up of Judges, Lawyers and a lay person to scrutinize such issues as had just developed. Yet Shaan undertook this role as a vital task to establish an invited investigative and advisory roll the function of which was not only to assess the issue and make recommendations but critically to regain the confidence in the judiciary by the public.

Nonetheless a follow up meeting within the hour was arranged with the Chief Judge of the Circuit, Dale Ross. Judge Ross had been the Chief Judge of the circuit for 12 years and counting – and his daughter had been appointed as a Magistrate in the circuit as well. It rather seems that when you get into certain offices in Florida you entrench yourself and then pretend nepotism does not exist while it clearly gets practiced. The idea of an independent investigative and advisory role by the Commissioner was discussed. Other Administrative Judges, all appointees of Judge Ross were also invited to attend this meeting. In all the meeting lasted another hour – culminating in a written request and authority from the Chief Judge authorizing

Shaan to review this NHI incident, and interestingly also any other matters related to the circuit with respect to any other Human and Civil Rights issues. The Chief Judge simply asked Shaan to restore public confidence in the Judiciary and he said it writing. Again in retrospect this could be seen as walking into the Lion's Den, and poking the Lion hard in the eye. They don't like it.

After some weeks of investigation that involved interviews with witnesses to the comment made by Judge Greene, tracing the use of the acronym NHI and its historic roots – it finally emerged that in fact no wrong doing had occurred. The letter "N" in NHI had no reflection of any ethnicity, creed, religion or racism. NHI stood for "No Humans Involved" The argument was that the homicide was so heinous that the Judge used the term NHI to reflect his sentiments that it was beyond all reasonable contemplation how such acts of violence could actually occur – in the human race. Ironically it seemed that this particular judge was expressing his human disgust at murder and corruption, at which the media had made hay, inflaming passions and citing racism where it did not exist. The systemic corruption in other parts of the judicial system were somewhat side-lined by this particular case. In turning over some of the stones however it seems that Shaan had managed to possibly make some more enemies. However he had also demonstrated how he and the Commission could work and improve relations between the Judiciary and the people.

So from this incident many things resulted. In time public confidence was restored somewhat. The Commission formally organized a training programs specifically for Judges on matters of Human Relations. New elections within the Judiciary brought about changes in the Administrative Judge positions and indeed the Chief Judge position itself. Judge Dale Ross was replaced by election by Judge Victor Tobin.

As this matter involving the judiciary was drawing to a close other issues by concerned citizens started to filter into Shaan's office. Issues were expansive and at times involved allegations of wrongdoing of persons in positions of public trust. Most could be discounted as disgruntled persons simply wanting to air their frustrations or suppositions. Still other allegations although circumstantial yet seemingly plausible were simply beyond the authority of Shaan's office as Commissioner for Human and Civil Rights. Some of what was said for actions of corruption would show the legitimacy of their color in time – unfortunately at the time not soon enough for Shaan. In an atmosphere of distrust, political machinations and corruption it was always difficult to tell who was friend and who was foe.

"A New York Minute"

Shaan's activities in the public sphere had caught the attention of South Floridians that continued to have ties to New York. Understandably many New Yorkers end up vacationing and retiring in the Sunshine state (Florida). Florida at a time was so awash with New Yorkers it was sometimes referred to as the 6th Borough. Through other acquaintances and connections Shaan was invited to New York City by the then Chief of Police of Seagate, New York, Robert Abraham (known as Bobby). Bobby had retired from the New York Police Department (NYPD) as a Inspector and then taken on this new post as Chief of Police at Seagate, a small rather exclusive suburb out at the end of a promontory. Bobby was in his late fifties with gray hair and always immaculately attired. He had always had close ties to the Chinese community and had an unforgettable accent in his speech when he spoke English to those from the Chinese community. It was not acceptable practice from a Human Relations perspective but it seemed to work for him and those he communicated with. Seagate is located at the end of Cooney Island and as Shaan would come to learn was an unusual type of small municipality. It was a kind of hybrid of a homeowners association and a municipal type of government – most unusual and likely the only such type of entity anywhere in the United States. It was a somewhat closed community and it had its own Police Force, - a Mayor and Council. Even in this quite well-heeled area post 9 /11 they started to see a rise in instances of hate crimes and of hostility and abuse within its community. Shaan, because of his experience, was requested to come and survey the situation and make appropriate recommendations. He provided services to Seagate without remuneration – it was a matter of acting for the benefit of the overall community and society. Programs of community policing and integrated community activities were created and recommended for implementation. Seagate for their part put Shaan through a Peace Officer certification program and then awarded him the rank of Deputy Chief of Police (Honorary). In the course of several visits to New York / Seagate, Shaan had several meetings with Law Enforcement Executives that included the NYPD Commissioner Ray Kelly, Chief of Department Esposito and US Marshall for the Eastern District of New York Gene Cochran. Through his visits to the New York City and meetings he had with various Senior Law Enforcement Executives, Shaan's interest in areas of security of special interest assets grew. His interest was piqued when he reflected on his time in the Naval Reserves, his observation of security New York and the vital assets of Florida ports to the national interest. Florida boasted critical points of entry at the airports and seaports, and the security issues were many and complex. Eugene Cochran, United States Marshall for the Eastern District of New York would write to Shaan - "Securing America's ports and transportation resource is a vital role for all public safety agencies as part of their Homeland Security responsibilities. Your initiatives in exploring methods that would provide enhanced integration of security systems at Florida's seaports, airports, railways and terminals is an enlightened and worthwhile endeavor. … Please be assured of my continued support … "

Many of them would write to the Governor of Florida commending the work the Florida Commissioner was doing in New York.

One person of distinction and special note that Shaan met during this time was Anthony Whitaker. He had been a Captain and Watch Commander at the Twin Towers on that fateful morning of September 11, 2001. Anthony would ultimately retire from the Department as a 3 star Chief in charge of aviation. Basically, this meant that every major airport in the New York / New Jersey was under his watchful responsibility. The two men hit it off in friendship from their first meeting. They shared many discussions on professional public safety matters and also on personal aspects of their lives. Anthony shared with Shaan that he simply could not remember nearly 80 percent of that morning of 9/11 – perhaps to save himself from the psychological anguish. Anthony had ordered in many of the men into the Towers to rescue civilians – and many of those he had ordered in would not come back out again. This was a major burden carried on the conscience of man who cared, and felt responsible for his men. Two of the men he ordered in that morning who had not come back out again he had trained with in the academy – they were particular friends, and it was and continued to be a heavy cross to bear. Like many others involved with those tragic events the scars cut deep and the psychological effect were permanent, often being likened to the guilt of those who survive wars when many didn't.

Anthony and Shaan would speak frequently over the phone, often about security ideas but also just touching base. One afternoon while Shaan was in his office Anthony called to say, mysteriously, he was having a package posted by registered mail – and he said it was important and that it required Shaan's attention immediately on delivery. Anthony did not inform Shaan what was in the parcel – when asked he simply said he could not discuss it but that it was important that Shaan see it as soon as possible on its arrival. The clear impression was that the parcel contained confidential policy or procedures in consideration of port security or emergency responses, matters which had been a matter of intense discussion between the two men. When the parcel arrived a few days later it was unusually heavy and the size of the box did not suggest that it contained documents. With care, and trepidation, and completely intrigued, Shaan sliced open the parcel. In it Shaan found, to his complete surprise, a block of steel that had been recovered from the World Trade Centre Tower 1, and it was inscribed and attested to as being from the attack on 9/11. When Shaan opened the parcel he was standing –when he saw what was in it – and he slowly and silently sank into his chair it – and a cold chill ran up his spine – it was a gift too powerfully valued, and emotions ran high, and words were silenced. These events had such a symbolic importance in American life and to be involved with them in this way was deeply significant to Shaan, as an American. After a few moments of reflection Shaan picked up the phone and called Anthony. Shaan asked – "What can one say to a gift like this?" – Anthony simply responded by saying he "wanted to share it with a soul that would understand". This coming from the man who was the New York New Jersey Port Authority Captain in charge of the Towers on 9/11 and was nothing less than the recognition of kindred souls. It made Shaan feel as though he had been made a blood brother in the brother in the 9/11 law enforcement fraternity fraternity.

Commissioner Shahrukh Dhanji (Shaan) and Chief of Aviation Anthony Whitaker, NY/NJ Port Authority Police Department.

Commissioner Shahrukh Dhanji (Shaan) and
Commissioner Ray Kelly NYPD

Chapter 4. *Call to Candidacy – The House is Dirty.*

"A lie gets halfway around the world before the truth has a chance to get its pants on" - Sir Winston Churchill

---

This is how Carl Hiaasen, the novelist and satirist describes Florida: "The Sunshine State is a paradise of scandals teeming with drifters, deadbeats, and misfits drawn here by some dark primordial calling like demented trout. And you'd be surprised how many of them decide to run for public office."

The stench of the cesspool that filled the political air in Broward County was screaming for a breath of fresh and clean air. Someone had to clean-up the political pollution.

And so, 'Shaan" – Shahrukh Dhanji decided to run for the chief public safety office in the county – Sheriff. The difference was he was running for all the wrong reasons, like community service, attempting to improve the way that the administration worked, and to drive out corruption. Someone should have told him that swimming with sharks was a risky business.

The Broward county Sheriff's office had historically been undermined by compromised leadership. It is arguably the most powerful constitutional office in a county of 2 million residents, and potentially one that exerts significant policy and public safety influence throughout the state. It protects Port Everglades, a vital strategic interest – which is the deepest seaport south of Norfolk, Virginia that can dock major capital Navy and Merchant ships.

When Shaan was serving as Commissioner, Ken Jenne was a member of the political elite of Florida and had served in the state Senate. He was an attorney, not a man of impressive stature or charisma, short and bald but with plenty of political savvy. He had been appointed by the Governor of Florida to be Sheriff in Broward County, when the serving Sheriff had passed away during his term. Jenne was later elected to the position of Sheriff when his appointed term ended. When he arrived at the Sherriff's office Jenne started to have his name labelled on all department assets, this was a politician who took himself seriously. Then his name was incorporated into the design and seal of the Sheriff's badge on patrol vehicles, letterhead, you mention it, if there was a Sheriff Seal on anything at all - Jenne's name was incorporated into it. This marketing campaign attempted to have the person and the office merged, as though they were inseparable and natural. This kind of personalization had never happened before- and at the time hardly anyone took objection as it developed into a glaring reality. Every patrol car was patrolling its zone as an advertising billboard for the individual who was the officeholder.

Imagine having the individual name of the President of the United States printed on every military aircraft, military vehicle and naval vessel– an absurdity at any level for any office holder to abuse their office in this manner. It was just comical and yet no one really questioned it from a legal perspective, let alone the waste of tax dollars or the sheer foolishness of it all. This was the slippery skin of the underlying "Banana Republic Dictatorial" mentality- maybe he was just playing Napoleon in Broward County, Florida. (interestingly, Broward County was created in the early 1900s from parts of Miami-Dade County and Palm Beach County, during the term of then serving governor Napoleon Bonaparte Broward)

The strange things that happened during Jenne's term in office in time started to unsettle the old boy's network of politicians in South Florida including Broward politics to various degrees. In his second term in office Jenne came under a Federal Investigation that alleged he was taking bribes. A Federal Grand Jury was eventually convened. The investigation went on for a long time and dragged on taking up many months if not over a year. Finally the Sheriff, Ken Jenne was indicted. He was arraigned at the Federal Courthouse in Ft. Lauderdale, Florida and on a pre-arraigned plea deal he served out his term with an early release in various Federal Facilities – mostly thought as easy confinement facilities. When he came back to Broward County he was, bizarrely, offered and accepted a position with the law firm headed up by one Scott Rothstein. Rothstein, it turned out was the Bernie Madoff of Florida. Within a year of Jenne going to work for Rothstein, Rothstein was investigated arrested and sentenced in the same Federal Courthouse as Jenne. Interestingly, Mike Satz the Circuits State Attorney failed to participate in the Jenne investigation or prosecution, took campaign contributions from Rothstein, and Rothstein's friends, partners and colleagues – in both instances Satz as the State Attorney was absent from the investigation or the prosecution when the very opposite was required by duty of his office. Rothstein, who is now disbarred, was at the time a prominent lawyer in South Florida, with his main office in Ft. Lauderdale, Florida. His law company Rothstein, Rosenfeld Adler, also now defunct, was one of the largest in Florida. His political connections were considerable, influential and costly to donate too, which he did on a large scale.

Rothstein was accused, charged and found guilty in Federal Court and sentenced to 50 years incarceration for orchestrating a $1.4 Billion dollar Ponzi scheme. Like Madoff, Rothstein was plausible, persuasive and knew everybody in Florida. Rothstein was the managing shareholder, chairman, and chief executive officer of the now defunct Rothstein Rosenfeldt Adler law firm. He was accused of funding his philanthropy, political contributions, law firm salaries, and an extravagant lifestyle through his Ponzi scheme – which evolved into his full time professional practice and performance. His Confidence tricks - the game – the “Con” is considered to be the 4th largest financial fraud since the first documented flimflam in 1719 involving Scotsman John Law. It was particularly audacious and yet also simple, like all Ponzi schemes relying on the greed of investors.

Rothstein's “Ponzi” was to pitch to investors the purchase of fabricated "structured settlements," in which people sell large settlements in legal cases for lump sums of cash, and the investor supposedly later collects the settlement. The investor was guaranteed a minimum of 20 percent investment returns in as little as three months

.

Like all Ponzi schemes this was one great big illusion which simply depended on getting more and people in to generate money – and eventually it crashes when there no suckers left. This great story has been well told by Chuck Malhus in ***The Ultimate Ponzi*** (2013) in which “Lawyer Scott Rothstein, in a breathtakingly ambitious Ponzi scheme, stole $1.4 billion to finance his opulent lifestyle. In this story of blackmail, betrayal, mafia, and murder, no one is innocent.” Naturally the Sherriff of Broward County at the time the scheme was going on was a friend of Rothstein’s and wrote him a letter congratulating him on winning libel actions against people who pointed to his nefarious activities.

How it worked was described by one insider in at least one instance was when unlicensed general counsel David Boden working with Rothstein who pitched the swindle – the “Con”. Rothstein meets and greets the investor and informs them that his firm was the preeminent sexual harassment law firm in the country. He says he'd figured out a basic formula which was that someone with $10 million net worth was usually willing to pay $2 million in cash to pay off their mistress. There was clearly plenty of sexual harassment that went on and Rothstein basically claimed to be profiting from it. The key to all of it was confidentiality. Rothstein tells the investor that he would meet potential defendants in his office and would question them about affairs they had with an employee. The defendants often would deny it. He pointed to artwork, and said there was a television screen behind it. He tells the investor he turned on a video of the guy having sex with his mistress, and told his client "We can either settle this now, or I can depose your wife, your mistress, you and your son about it." Since defendants" often couldn't or wouldn't pay the entire settlement up-front, Rothstein tells the investor that his first harassment case many years ago, involved a $3.5 million settlement and a million-dollar legal fee, so Rothstein assigned the settlement to a good friend and the plaintiff settles for $3 million without a trial. The "good friend" stood to be paid $3.5 million once the defendant paid up, a half-million dollar profit. The beauty of all this was, of course, that no-one should ever talk about it in public, the perfect cover.

"In 20 years, I have never seen a defendant sue on breach of settlement," Rothstein told them. "The whole idea is that it's secret. Why would they sue?"

Although it did not appear completely legitimate, and it might have appeared that the plaintiffs were short-changed, it made sense to the potential investor. The idea seems solid, and with little risk, particularly since Rothstien's company seemed solid and respectable. The investor thinks that with enough of these cases at Rothstein's law firm, they would be able to make huge sums of money, and it is the greed that is the magic charm in these schemes. Rothstein then continues to tell the investor about a potential allegedly fabricated case where investors would buy whistle-blower million dollar settlements with a sixty percent short term investor profit. The arrangement would be completely secret; the investor would never know the name of the company or the whistle-blower. The settlement money would be deposited into a trust account at TD Bank, accessible only to the investor at the appropriate time. The second in command David Boden follows up with all the questions and negotiates the contract with the targeted investor. Rothstein made a great play of the secrecy and even had a hidden lift that he would take clients into in order to impress them with the delicacy of his operations. Political connections and respectability were all part of the overall act. In the harsh light of day it all seems so ludicrous, but when people want to believe, they do.

Rothstein's connections with the Broward Sherriff's office came out later in court testimony. "Fort Lauderdale Ponzi schemer Scott Rothstein testified about how he had used the Broward County Sheriff's office as his personal police force under Republican Sheriff Al Lamberti. He said he also had inappropriate influence over local law enforcement, including sworn members of the Broward Sheriff's Office and Fort Lauderdale police department" (Broward Bugle 12/04/2014)

Discussing the kinds of inter-locking corruption and political back-scratching that went on in Florida brings us back to another important figure, Mike Satz, the Chief Prosecutor. Many Critics for years have labeled Broward County State Attorney Mike Satz as soft on public corruption. Something of course he denies. However there was so much dirty business in the Chief Prosecutors Broward backyard and he would just arrange cover for his favorites. A local investigative reporter Bob Norman wrote in 2009, "Satz isn't just close to the corrupt machine that runs Broward County, he is part of it."

Satz has been State Attorney since Gerald Ford was President of the United States. A prominent Attorney by the name of Mancini asked a particularly pertinent question regarding SATZ - "What I'd like to know, is why he hasn't filed a single prosecution from the Scott Rothstein - Ponzi scheme? Yet he took money from Scott Rothstein in 2007 for his campaign. Police officers were providing prostitutes to Rothstein's clients. That's a state crime that Satz should be prosecuting. Police officers are dealing drugs. That's a state crime that Satz should prosecute. Apparently Mike Satz doesn't see very much that goes on, he doesn't hear very much and he certainly doesn't prosecute very much."

In a notable instance Satz again failed to act where there seemed to be rancid corruption in the School Board. In fact State Attorney Satz's office ran a years-long grand jury to investigate School Board corruption during the 1990s, finding all kinds of dirt but oddly failing to file any criminal charges. Noting this failure and several probative indicators the FBI conducted a sting operation and nabbed State Attorney Satz's political ally and School Board Member Beverly Gallaghar. She retained the same political consultant as Satz, a certain Barbara Miller. Miller and Satz clearly worked hand in hand insuring that the shared political clients of Miller are always protected or at least given preferential treatment when there was criminal legal scrutiny. This kind of activity in turn helps Satz to continue his invisible hand of control and influence on the pulse of politics that could have any effect on him or the elected in his support network.

According to the FBI complaint, Gallagher schemed to steer a School Board construction project to a company called Pirtle in order that Pirtle could then give subcontract work to a company represented by the FBI agents, unbeknownst to Gallagher. She, according to the complaint, told the FBI agents she could arrange with her influence that Pirtle would get the contract. When the School Board sub-committee met and voted granting Pirtle the contract, their lobbyists Neil Sterling and Barbara Miller sat in the audience. In fact Barbara Miller was not only Pirtle's Lobbyist, but also Gallaghar's political consultant – just as she was for Satz. Gallaghar rigged the sub-committees vote to insure that Pirtle would get the contract – all for a pay-off that was part of the FBI's sting operation investigating the School Board.

The Feds allege that Gallagher told them she spoke to two men whose votes were necessary to go the way she wanted and had promised instructing them to vote for. One of the men would do what she wanted as he mistakenly believed he owed her his job as Hollywood Hills School principal. For rigging the vote, undercover agents paid Gallagher $6,000 in cash, according to the complaint. The feds allege that Gallagher, in all, accepted $12,500 in bribes, some of which she stashed in her own doggy bag at a restaurant. These small amounts hardly seem worth the effort – but it just reflects how corruption was institutionalized and as normal as breathing air.

It is clear that Satz's invisible hand of influence in control remains entrenched. When you have been the State Attorney for 40 years – it is not inconceivable that somehow a file is created on just about everybody that is somebody, just like Hoover and the old FBI, knowing the secrets gives you power. In fact a State-Wide-Grand-Jury on corruption was about to come down on Satz, because of his 30-year history of shielding, protecting and defending corruption. Because of Satz, Broward County has become a cesspool of corruption and incompetence. Satz was in the cross-hairs when, for some unknown and unexplained reason, Shapard and the other AAG (Assistant Attorney General Florida) sent down from Tampa to lead the Grand Jury investigation were fired. He breathed easily once again.

It was in the light of these influences and entrenched political deviance –real and perceived that Shaan was asked by some community leaders to consider running for the Democratic nomination for Sheriff of Broward County. The office and the credibility of law enforcement necessitated and required restoration and political change. Once again however this was a big call and dangerous mission, the Sherriff was a powerful person. The Sheriff's office annual estimated budget is in excess of 700 Million USD. The scope of services is expansive that includes but is not limited to:

Public Safety
Law Enforcement
Detention
Fire Rescue
Paramedic Services
School – Human Resource Officers
Port Protection (Sea and Air)
Child and Family Protection Services

With such a broad and important responsibility to individuals and to the community, which also required fiscal sensibility, the role of Sheriff was strategically key. Broward County boasts 2 million residents and also represents the most culturally diverse county in the state of Florida. The answer to all of the issues of concern seemed simple – and logical – to run for the Democratic nomination for Sheriff.

Governor Jeb Bush with Commissioners. Commissioner Shahrukh Dhanji third from left.

Chapter 5. *The Campaign*

"You're only going to find out who your real friends are when you get through a campaign and see who is still standing next to you" – Howard Gressman

---

Shortly after Shaan had completed his investigation of the "NHI" incident in respect of Judge Charlie Greene it was becoming very clear that Sheriff' Jenne's Federal indictment was imminent. When it finally did come as a result Jenne was removed from office. The Governor appointed Al Lamberti, a long serving law enforcement executive to complete Jenne's unfinished term in office. Ken Jenne spent only a year in federal prison for corruption, as he had done a plea - bargain. Even after being sent down for corruption there were those, like the aptly named journalist Buddy Nevins, who supported him saying: "I know he is controversial I've heard for years he can be vengeful against political enemies. Mean-spirited and nasty. Still, I think he has accomplished a great deal for Broward County. His imprint is on the university system, the roads, public safety and even our commission form of government." (Broward Beat.com) This sounds like the commentator who once said of a famous gangster "when he wasn't killing people he was a really nice guy". Jenne of course went on to work for the prolific fraudster Scott Rothstein, and perhaps he was just often misunderstood.

Because of Shaan's community involvement and track-record talk about the possibility of him running to be the next Sheriff started to circulate in some circles. He was a Human Rights Commissioner with integrity, a businessman with a law degree and also prior service in the Naval Reserve, all of which seemed more than sufficient to put up a viable and winnable candidacy. Basically there was a real, perceived need to put up an honest candidate who might be able to reform the chronically corrupt Broward County. A loosely formed committee of organizers started to form – which ultimately made the possibility of the candidacy real. From here on in Shaan was going to find out who his friends really were.

On a late Sunday morning at home with his wife and children, Shaan sat the family down and discussed the possibility of a campaign. He knew that it would take its toll on the family and he wanted them to try and understand what he was going to do. Perhaps the children were young, too young – a daughter 8 and son 9, but Shaan wanted to try and engage them in the process. He wanted to keep them informed – to express and give value to their opinions thoughts and decisions. The American experience in all its various colorful threads that weave together in the democratic process was something Shaan wanted his children to feel and touch from as early an age as possible. With adoring eyes both son and daughter endorsed their father –"Dad go for it". His wife also provided her dutiful support and encouragement. It seemed to be a good idea and one that would be a sensible extension of Shaan's community work and contacts, this was America where anyone could be President, let alone Sherriff of Broward County.

So with his family in support – Shaan and his group of supporters and colleagues who had ushered him into campaign mode needed to find an experienced, knowledgeable Political Consultant who understood the electoral terrain of Broward County. Somebody recommended a fellow by the name of David Brown, who was checked out and then consulted. David graciously accepted the invitation to meet. The meeting occurred at a restaurant in north Fort Lauderdale on Cypress Creek road. At the meeting with Shaan, were two of his main supporters, Keith Roberts and Howard Gressman. It was a long lunch and an intense discussion. David Brown offered Shaan a warning that was somewhat prophetic – "they will come after you and they will look to destroy you". This was simply because Shaan was seeking a constitutional office that is powerful, it controls a budget of 700 million, and, although supposedly open to anyone, you are the outsider. But Brown went on to say that Shaan might be just what was needed in the murky waters of Florida politics, a clean public servant who was not seen as the usual politician from the same

Old Boys network. After all it was also the time when Obama was running in the primary and he had already started to garner support. In Dave Brown's thinking then if Obama, why not Shaan – the classic American-Immigrants story, someone who had served his country in the military, been successful in business and served the state as a Commissioner. On paper Shaan was perfect, he had a strong academic background and he had business connections and was savvy. Dave Brown left the lunch with an understanding – he would take on Shaan's candidacy in the Primary for nomination for Sheriff on behalf of the Democratic Party. Dave also had the notion that he needed to come up with a catchy name for the campaign and the candidate. Some weeks later the campaign identity was unveiled by Brown and it ran "Shak for Sheriff". It was a kind of branding that Shaan was not particularly comfortable with but he acquiesced to Brown's expertise and experience in the matter – and so the campaign began. The "Shak" brand for the campaign was born, and actually it is probably rather catchy and might well have worked, had it been an open election.

It all began very well, as community and condominium leaders, and local city elected officials started to hear of Shaan's intention to run under the "Shak for Sheriff" banner, the campaign started to acquire significant endorsements and momentum. Through daily grassroots stumping as more and more of the platform message was heard local grass roots support started to rise. It took lots of community meetings, neighborhood walks – knocking on doors, Breakfast and Prayer meetings, Community centers, sponsored lunches, and Democratic Club meetings and dinners.

Shaan's platform message deliberately broke from the traditional candidacy stump speeches of the importance of fighting crime and ensuring high arrests or of praising badge wearing and gun toting deputies. His campaign was about assessing the community's different needs as a whole, and about crime prevention and community policing. Shaan wanted to measure real crime fighting by thinking about how to decrease crime and not the usual "lets fill up the jails." Interestingly in the last decade American states have started to realize that prisons cost far too much and that locking up thousands of people leads to bankruptcy. Like Shaan's campaign to prevent crime by creating platforms of better community and law enforcement partnerships, it has become clearer that prevention is better than detention. The proposed programs included creating mentoring programs with students, Sheriff office deputies and other public safety officers; and creating a volunteer Chaplain corps that would provide assistance and counselling to those impacted by domestic violence, or other incidents where just having a chaplain there would aid the victim. One of the platform ideas went so far as to promote Green cars for non-emergency use within the auto fleet of the Sheriff's office. This was an up-dating of crime fighting politics for the 21st century, not just the standard line used time and over of crime fighting and anti-corruption.

The office of Sheriff was actually a much wider position of public safety than simply crime fighting and more importantly it also cast a long shadow on many other social issues, certainly in the county and with considerable influence across the state.

One item of the campaign platform was the demand that deputies have at least a 2 year Associates Degree as opposed to the current High School diploma or equivalent. The practice of take home cars which had become the standard norm would continue with the adjustment that the program eligibility would only be if the deputy resided in Broward County. There is no point in parking a police car in the driveway to show your presence in the effort to deter crime, if the car is not parked in a driveway of the home county. Shaan wanted Broward tax money in every respect to stay in the county. These were unconventional steps – but they made good and common sense to most of the people listening.

Along the campaign trail people would come up to volunteer and help out. A few volunteered their time on a full time basis. There were those who were God sent, people like Lew Fromkin, a private businessman and family man who cared about community and gave of his time, participated in private fundraising events and acted as representatives when it was not possible for Shaan to be in more than one place at a particular time. But like all good things there also comes the dark side. There were people who wanted to infiltrate the campaign as scavengers and barracuda's. The latter was best exemplified by Nadezdha Martinez- she would later be recognized as one of the Agents of Political Cancer, one of three who were clearly, in retrospect, planted in the campaign. Nadezdha had been the former secretary to the Chair of the Democratic Party in Broward County, Mitch Ceasar. She approached Shaan at a dinner held by the Dolphin Democratic Club in Ft. Lauderdale. She offered her services to the campaign as a volunteer. Shaan in passing conversation said he welcomed all the help that could muster and that they could meet at another time in the coming week to discuss her support. Nadezdha finally came on board first as a volunteer – then demanded a salary from the campaign. It became rather a sticky situation. The campaign was not modeled to pay an entourage of staffers – it was modelled to be a grassroots campaign supported by volunteers with one remunerated Campaign manager. Not wanting to upset the apple cart of the campaign while in motion, Shaan came up with the idea of offering Nadezdha the opportunity to engage on a commission based position with one of his business interests. This would allow her to make an income and still be available to volunteer for the campaign. The next thing that occurred, and it was pure Florida, was that it also came to be known that while Nadezdha was still in Shaan's business and campaign office her husband was in jail on trial on a murder charge. Although this was no reflection on Nadezdha, and certainly whether he was guilty of not had no bearing or reflection on her as a person, it had not been mentioned. What also came as a surprise is that she had filed a case before the very commission that Shaan sat on. It is worth noting that as a commissioner Shaan was not involved in the all cases that were brought through the commission. As a commissioner his responsibilities and duties were to provide Policy and Direction to the commission and to serve as an adjudicator at hearings on cases concluded by the commission. This unforeseen problem came to a head when Nadezdha asked for Shaan's influence and interference in the case before his commission – she was expecting a rather sizeable settlement from the party she had filed charges against. Not being a typical Florida politician, Shaan refused. He pointed out that the case would be handled under the law on its merits.

It became clear that Nadzedha was heading for the exit from Shaan's campaign. She then went shopping for a position with other campaigns in the same political cycle – offering up concocted stories of the "Shak for Sheriff" campaign to increase her sales value. The media reporting of her departure from the campaign was damaging – what remained eventually more devastating was her ongoing communication and influence with two more campaign volunteer staffers, Darwish and Merolle – who were the other two Agents of Political Cancer. These people would also be dispensed with fairly soon within the development of the campaigns life cycle – but their activities and effects would link into the politically fueled investigation against Shaan. Questions about why they had volunteered had to be asked.

Many more volunteers came onto the campaign fold – and the campaign was gaining ground with support from community leaders, it seemed that there was a genuine movement to elect an outsider and to try and reform Broward County. Shaan's campaign was having a real effect and it was showing. Interestingly at the dinner where Shaan first meet Nadezdha the newly appointed Sheriff Al Lamberti was also present, he was the replacement for the imprisoned Ken Jenne. After the dinner Lamberti, Cooper City Commissioner John Sims and Shaan retired for a drink in the Hotel lounge where the dinner had been held. The men stayed and chatted for over an hour. Sheriff Lamberti declared in no uncertain terms that were the election today he would be out of job and Shaan would be the newly elected Sheriff. Commissioner John Sims was shocked to hear this admission from Sheriff Lamberti. Perhaps this was what set the alarm bells ringing in the drinking dens of the Florida political elite, outsiders could be very dangerous.

The support for the “Shak for Sheriff” campaign had started of strong – with lots of momentum. Over the course of the campaign one of the most notable supporters from the community were Gert Weinburg, 92 years of age at the time. She had been a former stage dancer in New York City. She had a fabulous career having also set up a dance school during her professional years. Now she was the de-facto Grand Madame of politics at Woodmont Condominium Association, this was a resident’s association of literally thousands of voters. A similar Grand Madame of a condominium association was Adele Berger of Century Village. Her husband had served in the US Navy – in a rather peculiar way it created a bond of friendship between Shaan and Adele. Both these ladies support for Shaan was unwavering and staunch. The best kind of loyalty in politics was exhibited by them. It was clear that ordinary voters really did want change and supported the anti-corruption ticket that Shaan was standing on. The similarity with Obama seemed quite strong, both total outsiders who initially seemed to have no hope, but only one of them was going to win.

As the campaign proceeded some elected officials who had also endorsed the “Shak for Sheriff” campaign, suggested Shaan contact and connect if possible with two other prominent county-wide political consultants, Vinnie Grande and Bev Stracher. Both of these well-known consultants came on board helping Shaan in what was arguably a first for them – on a strictly volunteer basis. Both gave their support and Bev Stracher even stood up to the media in defense of Shaan. Through various introductions many of the city commissioners from the 31 cities that comprise Broward County came to meet and get to know Shaan. A sizeable number of them gave him their endorsement. The most interesting city commissioner endorsement came from a Jules Schneider – at 93 he was the oldest serving city commissioner in the state. The campaign seemed to be going in exactly the right direction.

The race for the Democratic nomination for Sheriff was comprised of nearly 10 candidates. Towards the end there were only 5 still in the race. Shaan Dhanji, Scott Israel, Rick Lemack, Wiley Thompson and Bruce Udolf. One of the candidates that withdrew was Philip Sweeting, a former Deputy Chief of Police from Boca Raton. Shortly after he dropped out of the race he endorsed Shaan. No other candidate in the race had the privilege of being endorsed by a former candidate in opposition. This powerfully demonstrated Shaan's credibility, especially coming from a senior law enforcement executive. His campaign was strong and the opposition were beginning to recognize it. Once it became clear that Shaan well might win then the machine started to whirr and the attack to get the strongest horse out of the race began. In a corrupt society no one is more threatening than an honest person and the need to ensure an insider, part of the powerful political few, could win was absolute. As Helena put it in All's Well that ends well: "*Why then tonight let us assay our plot." (All's Well That Ends Well (III, vii, 43-44).* Unfortunately this did not end well for Shaan's campaign.

The attack did not only come from the outside, it had to come from within as well. Thus, as it turned out, just as the rhetorical slugging on the campaign trail started the hidden agents who were ready to undermine the "Shak for Sheriff" candidacy were already in place. If Al Lamberti, the appointed Sheriff of the Republican Party could see the political threat of Shaan as a winning candidate – then so did the few "powerful political people" and their nominees in the race. The agents of political cancer embedded in Shaan's campaign came under the guise of volunteers. By the time they were discovered it was too late. Those that were embedded were essentially discovered and separated from involvement by the end of the first quarter of the campaign. By then it was too late – the poison had infected the body of the campaign. These political barracuda's would do the bidding of the powerful political few, devastate the election process, make a mockery of the state's criminal justice system and get away with it – until now.

The wickedness of this plan would become clear in time – the puppet masters would be names to remember – the State Attorney Michael Satz, the Political Consultant

Barbara Miller and the opposition candidate Rick Lemack, former deputy Chief of the most historically corrupt Police Department in the state of Florida, along with his former colleague from Hollywood PD and now with the Florida Department of Law Enforcement (FDLE), Special Agent James Futch. He was the lead agent in charge of the investigation which targeted Shaan and the entire "Shak for Sheriff" campaign. This group of people, the hit-squad as it were, basically represented or were the nominees of the powerful political few. They in turn pulled the strings of influence and control over the scavengers purposefully embedded in the campaign as volunteers– Nadezdah Martinez, Elizabeth Darwish, Mike Merolle and an unusually useful bystander Tania Martinez-Green, who later turned witness in a made up affidavit in order to avoid her own prosecution. However, there also many people visited or interviewed by Agent Futch would still call Shaan, despite being told not to communicate with him or inform Shaan of the visit – who would report that Futch was on a "Witch-Hunt". People like Bill Faller, a colleague in the finance sector and Davis Revell, a business partner and Assistant Public Defender for the 2nd Circuit of Florida.

What was going on here was not just simple corruption – where a bribe or special favor was being passed or demanded. The acts undertaken by these people had a direct seismic impact on the fundamentals of a democratic election cycle that is the cornerstone of any republic– it was an act of internal terror. To subvert democracy is to subvert freedom, and there is no greater evil than this kind of democratic demolition.

"-.. the wicked are in glee when the good fail to pursue."
John F. Kennedy

A unanimous report was filed as reported initially by the FDLE (Florida Department of Law Enforcement) of financial irregularities in Shaan's campaign. This allegation came within days of Shaan getting rid of these so-called volunteers, the Agents of Political Cancer – the scavengers from his campaign. After these people were separated no further reporting surfaced. The investigation however persisted with timely releases to the Press and Media – fundamentally violative of internal FDLE's policy and practice, especially since the matter was only an allegation and its disclosure would affect the outcome of an election cycle. The mission was accomplished. The plot was to commence an investigation and to derail Shaan's campaign "Shak for Sheriff". Afterall who wants to elect someone under investigation by FDLE. It would take time but the wicked web once weaved would start to show itself with abundant visibility. For Shaan it would be the beginning of something beyond contemplation.

Shaan knew he could not now win the election, but he also understood he had to keep the fight going. Anything else would prove that the allegations made were well founded and his dropping out of the race would betray the supporters who had already come to his side.

Commissioner Shahrukh Dhanji (Shaan) as candidate seeking nomination from the Democratic Party with Sheriff Al Lamberti (Broward County) the Republican candidate

Chapter 6. *The Smoking Gun of Political Incest*

"...an animal, at the end of a few months, is what it will be all its life; and its species, at the end of a thousand years, is what it was in the first of those thousand years. Why is man alone subject to becoming an imbecile?"

— Jean-Jacques Rousseau, *Discourse on the Origin of Inequality*

It became abundantly apparent the way that politics has become imbecilic in general, and in the case of Florida, very specifically. We start with the State Attorney, Mike Satz, and with his political consultant and ally Barbara Miller, who also just happened to be Rick Lemack´s political consultant. Lemack was put up against Shaan Dhanji in the primary for the nomination of the Democratic Party in the race to be Sheriff. Lemack is a fellow of average height and build – soft spoken and not a man that exudes presence when he walks into room – he was fairly inconspicuous as a personality in many ways. One attribute Lemack did possess was a political ability of manoeuvring with shrewd stealth; he could somehow talk into complacency anyone in direct conversation with his non-attenuated tone of speech. Special Agent Futch´s wife volunteered and worked for Lemack´s campaign. Futch was a long-time friend and colleague of Lemack´s from their days together in the

Hollywood Police Department. To say that these people were working together to unseat Dhanji is a bit like saying that the sun shines in Florida. In fact, Futch volunteered to lead the investigation against Shaan Dhanji and concluded the investigation by asking the State Attorney's Office – Michael Satz (Broward County Florida) to issue an arrest warrant against Dhanji. An investigation first reported to have triggered based on an anonimous tip.

If the investigation was meant to be objective and clear of the appearance of any impropriety why would anyone allow an agent with these kinds of personal ties to people intimately connected to lead the investigation? Unless off-course the purpose of the investigation was not to be objective, but rather was clearly motivated by political factors and corruption. The answer to this question is as clear as the sunlight in Florida. It wasn't hidden either, for example the conversation of the then School Board member Beverly Gallagher is already known. She commented to Shaan, naturally over cocktails, after a Broward Days (a community based organization of business, community and political leaders) event at the Riverside Hotel in Ft. Lauderdale at the hotel bar – the reason he had lost the election was because he had the wrong Political Consultant. She also pointed out that she and Satz were very close, and that Shaan should speak to her to have Satz bury the investigation against him especially since the election cycle was now over. This was simply affirming what was clear, that there were indeed close ties shared amongst these people and that they lived and breathed together, not in the dark but in the full light of day. After all the State Attorney's office investigation into the scandalous School Board activities went nowhere and it was only the FBI that ultimately stepped in to investigate, which then also resulted in the arrest and conviction of Gallagher.

So the next step in the play was that Mr. Rick Lemack, a former Deputy Chief from Hollywood Police Department (PD) – (which just happened to be the most historically corrupt Police Department in Broward County, and indeed the state of Florida) – who decides to or is prompted to run in the Primary election for the Democratic nomination against Shaan. After leaving the Hollywood Police Department, Lemack interestingly got the post of Assistant City Manager for Hollywood. It turns out that the Hollywood Police Department has had and continues to have issues, little things like major and systemic corruption that went back at least into the 1980s. Lemack and Futch were both associated and a part of the Department at the same time. Since the 80's at different times the Department was investigated by the FBI, officers were arrested for providing services to organized crime – and a time when the serving Police Chief was removed. Old habits die hard, and in 2007, several Hollywood Police Department officers were implicated in a far-reaching corruption investigation by the FBI and some officers turned state's evidence in order to reduce their potential sentences. Four officers were jailed for the minor misdemeanor of trafficking in heroin. In 2009, five Hollywood Police Department officers were accused of trying to cover up a crash involving one of their own officers by lying on police reports. Officer Dewey Pressley is clearly heard on video saying he was going to "do a little Walt Disney here, " the report carries on with him saying, "if I have to bend the rules to protect a cop I'm gonna." The audio from the incident was recorded by dashboard camera, and was reportedly full of foul language, Walt Disney it was not. In 7 January 2010, Police Chief Chad Wagner fired the five officers involved in the incident, rather than charge them with corruption. The officers by that point were on their sixth month of paid leave. On 10 April 2012, Officer Joel Francisco was sentenced to ninety days in jail after he lodged a guilty plea in the original accident. He had been talking on his phone when he hit the other car with his official vehicle, something he forgot to mention. Pressley also arrested the woman whose car had been rammed (from behind) and claimed she caused the accident. Francisco's record showed eight traffic accidents in his twelve years with the department. Dewey Pressley, who was originally accused of felony conspiracy charges, which carry a thirty year sentence, ended up with less than two years behind bars. Throughout he had the support of the police union and other officers, who turned up in court to support someone who had lied, falsely arrested innocent people and tried to frame them. Another star of the Hollywood police department was Jonathen Commella who gave a brutal beating to a Hollywood man he mistook for a gun-waving suspect, it was just that it was completely the wrong man and he was totally innocent. Commella attacked and tasered Arben Bajra while he was handcuffed, after punching him the face several times as he arrested him. Bajra's skull was fractured in the attack and he suffered permanent impairment. Commella claimed he had mistaken Bajra for someone else, despite him looking nothing like the description of the suspect, and no charges were brought against the policeman, it was claimed he used “reasonable” force. In November 2013 the department paid Bajra compensation of $195,000, without admitting anything wrong had occurred. Commella naturally just moved on to another job, to be a deputy of the Broward County Sheriff.

So we come back to Special Agent James Futch of the FDLE, the man who volunteered to investigate Shaan, who was also a former Hollywood police department veteran and former partner to Lemack. So this candidate straight out of the swamp and running uphill in the political campaign against Shaan is suddenly supported by a politically conceived and instigated investigation lead by Lemack's longtime friend Special Agent James Futch. To add spice to the mix when Agent Futch's wife volunteers and works for the Lemack campaign for Sherriff, no conflict of interest there.

Although Lemack or Futch were never directly implicated in the investigations that affected so many others within the relatively small Hollywood Police Department, it is clear that to remain neutral in the clear presence of criminality is in effect to support that criminality. It is not exactly as though the levels of corruption in the department weren't known about, there was, in fact, massive media coverage. There is even a blog dedicated just to the topic, with the great title: *Rotten to the Core: Your One-Stop Shop for Hollywood Police Corruption (Bob Norman. July 30th 2009)*

He opens by saying:

"This latest Hollywood police scandal is only the most recent black spot on what I believe can now safely be considered the worst police department in America. The Hollywood department has been plagued with scandal for years, so I thought I'd develop a post that links past stories involving the department's corruption."

Lemack and Futch apparently never noticed anything the whole time they were there.

So State Attorney Mike Satz's (Broward) office issues a warrant against Shaan based on Special Agent James Futch's Probable Cause Affidavit based on the statements of witnesses. Of course Lemack and Satz used the same Campaign Manager Barbara Miller – who was also a Hollywood resident. Shaan's attorney, Richard Rosenbaum informs Satz's office of the close relationship between Futch and Lemack and of the obvious bias and impropriety of the investigation – and its probable effect on the political democratic process. Satz's office responded in line with their internal and insidious strategy by stating that they did not believe that the relationship had any influence on the investigation. This reminds one of Clinton's claim that he had never had "sexual relations' with that woman, whatever that meant.

Any balanced review of the correspondence from Satz's office, by his Deputy State Attorney Donelley, leads to a number of obvious questions. Why did the response on such an urgent matter take nearly a month? Generally responses are provided within a week, and in a matter so vital it should have been sooner. Clearly, Satz's office wanted to drag out the whole matter and give credence to the assertion that they knew of the relationship between the Investigator (Futch) , his wife (Debbie Futch) and the candidate running against Shaan, but that it was all "long ago". Quite what the importance in realistic, legal and quantifiable terms is of "long ago" is not explained.

One might ask how Satz and his deputy Donnelly were so sure that there was no influence in terms of these personal relationships on the investigation, unless Satz and Donnelly were themselves friendly with Futch and Lemack. There is the rather obvious point with Futch that his wife worked for Lemack in the campaign against Shaan, and they must share conversations in a spousal relationship. Why then when hundreds of other Agents were available for this investigation was Futch given the job or even allowed to volunteer for it when his personal connections pointed to complete and utter inappropriateness? The connections are so blindingly obvious, and so openly corrupt, knowing the depth of the personal relationships involved it produces so many conflicts of interest that no reasonable person would give it credence. So why was Futch given the investigation to handle against Shaan? – SIMPLY because it was not a legal investigation but a witch-hunt for blatant political purposes. Futch's investigation extended to nearly all of Shaan's business colleagues, partners and associates, and followed a well-worn path of suggestion, implication and innuendo. If there is an investigation there must be something needing investigation, and in business this is the kiss of death, because reputation is all. Since Shaan was standing on a campaign platform the included anti- corruption any whiff of problems was going to undermine the whole campaign. Exactly as intended this process starts to strangle and block the commerce ties in Shaan's business ventures and operations.

In violation of official FDLE policy and traditional practice leaks about the putative investigation continued to find their way into the media from Special

Agent Futch's office. One of Agents Futch's key witnesses is Mike Merolle, who was a Deputy Sheriff who had been with the Broward Sheriff's Office. A slow talking fellow with a low attenuation in his voice, he liked to purposefully put on an appearance of a fellow not to smart - but that was his manner. He ended up doing much better with people when they perceived him with lower expectations than his capability. He had done quite well alright on a Deputy Sheriff's salary and pension – he ended up owning about three properties in Florida and drove around in a classic red colored corvette. Merolle undoubtedly found himself psychologically emboldened by his connection to Futch and the illusive belief of impregnability and supremacy which came with being in a political power camp. Months after being removed from Shaan's campaign he asked for and a got a meeting with Shaan. The meeting happened at a site selected by Merolle on the Thursday afternoon before the July 4, 2008 holiday weekend. The meet happened in the parking lot of Po Folks Chinese restaurant. It wasn't a restaurant frequented by Shaan, in fact it was the first time he had been there. It was located in the southwest corner of a busy and main intersection of University Drive and Griffin Road in Broward County. The two first met inside, each ordered a drink and carried it out into the parking lot to have the conversation, which said something about the sort of conversation it was going to be. The conversation skipped over any civility or pleasantry and launched straight into a warning and a threat directed at Shaan.

In clear and no uncertain language Merolle declared that Shaan would suffer physical harm unless he got out of the campaign. Merolle carried on like some TV mafiaso in what Shaan saw as a comical but desperate attempt by an opposition camp that still perceived him as a viable political threat and legal opponent. Merolle went on to point out that Lemack was going to win the race and that Shaan should be more concerned about the well-being of his family, in the nicest possible way. The next line was that if Shaan did not quit – it was certain that he would not get his day in court as he simply would not be around. Merolle also further stated that Futch has already been instructed by Satz to clean-up the details and to bring Shaan down. Shaan's slightly surprised response in a few words in this brief but rather intense meeting was – 'this is not 1930's Chicago – and this is still the United States where it is the law that prevails' - and this was the last time he would see or entertain any calls from Merolle. Interestingly enough it was Merolle who first told Shaan about an investigation that was targeting him – well before the investigation was made public. How would he have known that before anyone else?

Elizabeth Darwish the other embedded agent of political destruction was a young newly graduated student from University with strong ambitions to get involved in local and state politics and to pursue a career in law. She volunteered to register all the campaign donations through a software program that is used to then file officially all contributions to the campaign with the office of the Supervisor of Elections. She was also provided with the only software license to download this software – which she does on her own personal laptop. The alleged improprieties of the campaign reporting originates from her registry and she simply refuses to surrender the reports or software when she leaves the campaign. Methinks I smell a rat, as someone said.

Most conveniently she then left Shaan's campaign to go and work on the campaign of another Barbara Miller client who is also running for re-election and shortly afterwards ends up working in Satz's office. He is the State Attorney who is the architect of the investigation being led by Futch against Shaan. He is the very man whose office will see and obtain the warrant for Shaan's arrest. Nothing could be more obvious about whom Darwish was actually working for. The weave of relationships and positions offered and acquired by these people in acts of treachery speak volumes of itself.

All issues that lay the basis for the investigation against Shaan occurred during the first quarter of the campaign. Once Mike Merolle, Elizabeth Darwish and Nadezdah Martinez, were thrown out of the campaign there existed no new basis or issue for any investigation. Coincidence? They all ended up working for Lemack, a Barbara Miller client or obtained a clear financial beneficial relationship. The only non-political witness was Tania Martinez-Green who was maneuvered into fabricated testimony to avoid charges being laid against herself. She was an unforeseen gift, pliable and useful. It also seemed that during the course of the investigation Futch and Merolle appeared to have developed an overly friendly relationship where the two openly discussed the investigation (which should have been confidential). Merolle was one of the three embedded political agents who had been thrown out of the campaign. Futch and Merolle were simply birds of the same feather who found each other through the web of this planned and corrupt investigation.

The unfortunate witness of circumstance, who was maneuvered into use was Tania Martinez–Green. She simply found herself put into a position to commit perjury on a sworn affidavit under manipulated and contrived conditions provided by Agent Futch. He gave Tania the path to escape from possible criminal prosecution for identity theft and financial fraud at the cost of her conscience, and just as heavily at the cost of tearing at the fabric of democratic ideals and assassinating the electoral process. Tania's claims in her Futch created affidavit were controverted by independent affidavits from employees of WACHOVIA bank – the institution where the wrongdoing was alleged to have occurred. Futch off course never took any of these independent affidavits or evidence into his case file.

The delightful Tania Martinez - Green had come to Shaan through a referral of some common acquaintances. Tania it transpired had recently been discharged from her position in the mortgage division of Chase Bank. She was a single mother of two and was working hard to provide for her children's welfare and university education. She also very badly needed to make money – since she had just been left unemployed. Shaan, acting in the trusting way that was his strength and weakness, had given her a job.

Shaan suggested she consider working as an independent affiliate of a company he had some personal interest in that was involved in the mortgage and lending industry. The name of the company was Antrim Mortgage - the name "Antrim" originated from a US Navy ship Shaan had served on. Tania did not however formally affiliate with Antrim. She did welcome any contacts in the banking and lending industry that she could be introduced to and affirmed that upon any deals being closed from introduction or contacts provided by her she would gladly remit back a referral fee to Antrim.

At this time Shaan was curtailing his business activities in order to continue to give a full effort to the campaign. He introduced Tania to contacts for commercial lines of credit and personal loans and mortgages at Wachovia bank – through one Sarah Dolfinger, who was the connection at WACHOVIA bank. Essentially Tania had a customer that needed a line of credit from the bank and so she went to Dolfinger to acquire the necessary paperwork – checklist and forms that the client needed to complete. She brought back all the necessary documents which were signed and submitted them to Sarah, who had never met the client and this was a an absolute violation of standard Banking policy, regulations and most certainly the Patriot Act as it applied to the banking industry. As it happened the identity of the client seeking the credit line was based on identity theft. Sarah extended good faith to Tania, notwithstanding the regulatory guidelines only to be adversely compromised – not to mention the horrific effect on the person whose identity had been stolen. In was in this rather unfortunate manner Tania and Sarah worked directly together. Tania brought clients to Sarah at Wachovia bank without Shaan's involvement or direct knowledge. The client files were managed directly between Tania and Wachovia's representative, Sarah. Later Sarah in fact provided an affidavit confirming that Shaan had no involvement in Tania's clients file – all of which was nicely ignored or swept under the rug by the Futch investigation. The press simply reported the connection with Shaan – building on to the spice of the story and the information life line from Futch's office. It was one of those situations where the question of the facts really didn't matter as long as the papers were being getting sold.

Tania was working on a loan file she had originated where in fact significant misrepresentation occurred by her where one of the party's named in the involved loan alleged clear identity theft. The allegation against Tania was ultimately, and quite fictitiously, linked back, by simple acquaintanceship, to connecting with Shaan. When Futch was made aware of this loose and tenuous connection, he used it to construct a pattern of self-serving gain. He basically made a deal with Tania offering her the opportunity to avoid prosecution from charges in exchange for being a witness against Shaan, one of the oldest tricks in the book. The affidavits from the banks representatives confirming the lack of Shaan's involvement in this matter were simply never given consideration, for fairly obvious reasons.

The web of cross haired and triangulated political assassination was not only well constructed by the embedded agents of political cancer but was now re-enforced by an unsuspecting participant who was simply trying to save her skin at any cost – and until now she had.

It was clear that Satz had issued a complete and unequivocal directive to bring Shaan down. It was well-organized and aimed exactly at the Campaign's strength, the appearance of honesty.

Once the Warrant is issued and set for execution on Feb 11 - Futch and his team moved to Shaan's residence to arrest him. By some strange serendipity Shaan however is not at home, or in the state of

Florida, something Futch might have checked beforehand? Futch's stupidity in this action led to his extraordinary and totally self-incriminating e-mail to others where he writes:
"there are some rather powerful political people that would like to see this man [DHANJI] arrested."

The existence of this "investigation" had first come to light when Futch went to visit everyone who had donated to the "Shak for Sheriff" campaign. One of his visits was to the home of Shaan's business colleague and friend Howard Gressman. In fact each of Gressman's family members had contributed 500 USD, each. Futch went around asking the donors to identify the sources of the funds they had donated. There were, of course, no improprieties in these funds donated by the Gressman family members or anyone else for that matter. During the early course of the investigation an offer is made by Shaan's counsel to FDLE Special Agent Futch that Shaan is prepared to assist the investigation with full disclosure of any documents or statements – which was interestingly declined by Futch. It is slightly hard to understand why, when the target of the investigation is prepared to meet discuss and share information on any matter the lead investigative agent, he would decline the offer. In general it would seem important to any investigation to have the investigative target agree to cooperation. This initial offer would have saved the campaign from improper public disclosure and it certainly would have saved tax-payer dollars and FDLE resources. But it was always clear that the investigation was not for the purposes of law enforcement – it's main purpose was to create irreparable damage to the lead candidacy in the race – and that mission was accomplished.

It was years later after Shaan, through his lawyers in the United States, had made his protected status public and questioned the integrity and veracity of the corrupt investigation that had targeted him.

His attorney Richard Rosenbaum wrote to elected officials stating in part:

" It is critical to note, that at no time did our client take to hiding. He has been in his self-imposed exile over the past 4 and half years and made his whereabouts abundantly known through various means. It has taken him the better of 3 years to weave the various aspects of the case together to expose the full extent of the tainted investigation. It has taken an additional 15 months for the legal process to conclude providing him the Protection he now enjoys. He attempted to bring attention to this matter prior to seeking formal protection. He transmitted communication to then Secretary of State Clinton during her visit to India and posted material on the internet, in blogs, websites and social media. He has not ceased in his effort to expose the corruption that in his words is "cancerous in Broward County, Florida". As recently as six to nine months ago communication was established with the FBI - Miami District. This matter, based on the grant of Subsidiary Protection is now on the international stage. … The fact that a nation that reflects our ideals of democracy and provides a legal process similar to our own has determined that in granting my client protection, that something went terribly wrong in the Florida investigation of my client. The blatant intentional action by individuals in public trust in our criminal justice system that resulted in the charges being filed has struck at the core of our democratic electoral process, and must not be allowed to go unchecked nor allowed to repeat."

The circling of the wagons defense by the cowboy perpetrators came into immediate full force and effect. Shaan was pictured along with the article confirming his Protection status as provided by EU laws by the leading newspaper in South Florida, the Sun-Sentinel. In the article the spokesmen for SATZ confirmed that should Shaan attempt a return to the US he would be arrested immediately – they also went further to explain that the incriminating email - "there are some rather powerful political people that would like to see this man [DHANJI] arrested." – was simply a technique, a means of flushing out the defendant, whatever that meant.

Boy Oh Boy, if this does not insult one's intelligence – and is circular reasoning at its finest. This admission of "technique" is in itself a contradiction and an affront to any sensible person. First to call an investigative process a "technique" it must be established as an official agency operational policy, and (2) this can only result after it has been done several times over in several situations /investigations. In other words that it is an accepted, tried and agreed technique. This is clearly not the case and therefore, FDLE Agent Futch has again only continued to obstruct justice by failing to disclose his active participation in this politically targeted investigation. Any person not telling the full truth to a law enforcement officer in the course of a lawful investigation is chargeable with Obstruction of Justice, which is a felony. Therefore, this law makes this alleged "technique" by FDLE Agent Futch wholly untenable. Why would Futch have to create a lie as a law enforcement officer when the law is more than sufficient for him to illicit a truthful response from anyone he questions?

Like one article on www.floridagaenda.com reported – " ...Satz and his staff are just soft on political corruption and they pick and choose which politicians they go after depending on political pressures and career benefits." The power of office is to determine who that power should be used against, and the corruption of power is use it against innocent citizens.

Chapter 7. *The Perfect Storm*

"Gonna be a real frog-strangling turd-floater." — Charles Martin, *Chasing Fireflies*

The perfect storm started with the public disclosure in the Sun-Sentinel of the investigation by the FDLE with a news release which had the intended and desired effect. The thunderous impact was immediately felt in political shocks to the candidacy. Previously sought endorsements from local elected officials failed to appear and would now become near impossible. It became difficult to retain some endorsements that had already obtained. For example Coconut Creek City Commissioner Becky Tooley became one of the first to abandon ship. She was the epitome of the politician who fails for lack of principle and conviction only to find ease of position by the wind current of the moment – not even the day. Fortunately, other city commissioners like, John Sims of Cooper City, Barrington Russell and Jules Schneider of Lauderdale Lakes and Leonard Freund of Coconut Creek stood firm. What had been a powerful campaign was now in constant damage control mode. Now it wasn't about winning – it was about making it to shore, by staying afloat. Still Shaan had to keep up all the outward appearance of a candidate confident who could, and should win.

The incriminating article came out on the eve of a fundraiser being held at the home of Dr. and Mrs. Mohsin Jaffer. Mohsin is a well-respected physician and had known Shaan since his 20s, and they had worked together on several community projects targeting youth and senior citizens. For example one of their joint projects had included obtaining burial privileges for a specific immigrant and religious group that had no cemetery availability in Broward County. He knew Shaan as a man of integrity and character and did not flinch in his support to the very end of the entire battle. Mohsin had an understanding of the turbulence generated in politics and its effect on society having been raised in Kenya (east Africa) during it turbulent political era. Although the event went ahead, many of the high end campaign contributors called at the last minute to say they were unable to attend. They required assurances that the article was nothing more than a political ruse to undermine the "Shak for Sheriff" campaign. Although the event was well attended and some great words were said in support of the campaign by the host, and local elected officials in attendance, the event as a fund-raiser was unsuccessful. Mohsin and his wife Fauzia, who believed in Shaan, remained stalwart to the end. However, some other people committed to invitations for fundraising events started to evaporate. The campaign still had no shortage of people wanting to help. Lynn Drucker, a very active member in the Navy League whose son was in the sea cadets with Shaan's son was enthusiastic about lending her support – with volunteered time, contacts in the community – even helping with a fundraising activities. Her support was brutally brought to a halt – when she rather embarrassingly informed Shaan she was asked to withhold support of his candidacy by some "well-positioned" but unnamed people to whom she could not refuse. What was also interesting about Lynn's offer was that it had started to show engagement in the "Shak for Sheriff" Campaign not only with Democratic Party members but also with votes from Republicans. They wanted to see him win the Democratic nomination in the hopes he would then ultimately win the election for Sheriff, as many people wanted a clean Sheriff

But all this momentum was drawn to a screeching halt by the investigation and it being made public, the campaign was holed below the water-line and slowly sinking. However, Shaan still thought there was off-chance he might still win, despite everything. The candidate himself was tainted by the investigation but the platform message was bold, striking and made good common sense. If nothing else the campaign platform issues would start a debate, and had clearly struck a chord with the electorate, there was an awakening of issues which could only be good. In any event Shaan was convinced that the investigation was baseless - how much further could it go before it would be ended and shown to be irrelevant?

There was in any case sufficient momentum in the campaign by way of clear community support in key voting precincts – or so it was believed because those that influenced the vote in those precincts were still very strongly in support of his campaign. The political poison soon challenged their influence within these precincts however and their ongoing open support of Shaan began to be eroded by the media drip by drop.

All through the period of the campaign, every few weeks another carefully organized release of information would leak from the FDLE – it did not say anything new – but kept the story alive and kicking. The release of these leaks was professionally designed and orchestrated by the Powerful Political few for whom Agent Futch did his bidding as well as on behalf of his friend Lemack's candidacy to ensure the stalling of the "Shak for Sheriff" campaign. Lemack was the nominee of the "powerful political people" (at least as represent by the Satz-Miller team.) who wanted, and needed, a compliant candidate – a fellow that would play ball and be a part of the machinery without upsetting the applecart.

Shaan's lawyer – Richard Rosenbaum, Esq., in a bid to try and halt these damaging leaks, had sent a letter to Tim Donnelly, -Satz's deputy who had been placed officially in charge of this matter in the State Attorneys' office. In part the letter stated – "Finally, we are greatly concerned over the "leaks" to the media concerning the investigation. When I first spoke with Agent Futch about the investigation on 3/ 27/08 I was assured that FDLE was making no public comment concerning this investigation. Much to my surprise, the following day, an article appeared in a local newspaper with a press release from the press agent for FDLE. More recently, despite assurance from everyone involved, another article was released titled "Sheriff Candidate Under Investigation". We intend to look into the source of the "leaks" and trust that you shall instruct and all agents working on this case that there should be no release of information at this time." The Reply from the State Attorney Satz's office to this was deafening silence – it was simply ignored.

What was needed here was a non-traditional approach from a defense lawyer. An approach to initiate a launch of enquiries as to how these improprieties were enacted rather than the conventional strategy of to wait and see what the State Attorney's office comes up with, and then try and defend. This process however was not in the making – at that time.

As all media strategists know once the media frenzy had begun – it persisted, accelerated and even grew, exactly as planned. It got to the point of an article being written about Shaan's wife and her traffic record, which was not anything more extraordinary than anyone else's – except that it was Shaan' s wife's traffic history. It got to be more and more absurd - where the campaign platform concepts and the integrity of the person running for position were overshadowed by the demands and practices of the gutter press.

Somewhere along the way the fundamental rights of the First Amendment – that includes Freedom of Speech and of the Press got transformed where the responsibilities that went with the freedoms ended up in the swamp. There should be a sense of duty, of awareness, of the need to keep the public informed – to ask the probing questions and not merely accept the official statements. It's the fundamental basis of why there is freedom of press – to ask the difficult questions and not merely to become the parrot voice of what is being spewed out by the political machine. Like the press didn't ask why Sheriff Jenne was putting his name on everything and anything he could – as the Dictator of a "Banana Republic" would. No one asked the pertinent question then, and now again in the running of this investigation no one stopped to question the legitimacy of it, or about the recurring leaks of the investigation and its effect on the election cycle. The Color of the Law is a guise most perfect even when used by those most unscrupulous. But then this is when the Freedom of Press is most critical and vital to a free and democratic society – a society that is governed by the law and not by those persons in position of temporal power. The Press is powerful, and power can easily be misused, and the power to break an election campaign is a dagger pointed straight at the heart of democracy.

Despite vague assurances from the FDLE and others – there was no letting up. It is fundamental that during an election cycle an investigation remains out of the view of the public until it is concluded. This is done with the specific intent of ensuring that the election is free and fair and that allegations do not to have an influence on the election or the vote. An investigation by its nature is just that – an investigation – it is not a charge or a conviction, but as is well known the connotation of an ongoing investigations is that there is wrongdoing. There is no smoke without a fire is such an oddly powerful idea, and thus the suggestion is deemed sufficient to have adverse impacts on the election cycle. Hence government investigative agencies as a matter of practice and policy do not divulge ongoing investigations that commence during an election cycle –to do anything else would be appalling, anti-democratic and probably illegal. Welcome to Florida as the sign says!

Not only was the news of the investigation routinely leaked, it turned out that the investigation had no boundaries. Not only had it spurred the gutter press into endless sensationalism but it spread into in the lives of Shaan's wife and children, and their education. Bizarrely Agent Futch had subpoenaed the scholastic records of the children and the financial history of their tuition. The realms of this "investigation" had left all reasonable bounds well behind. The officials of the school were kind enough to keep Shaan and his wife informed, but it had affects. There were simply no bounds of decency left.

The fact that almost anybody can spark an investigation, and that malicious rumours are routinely spread, particularly in politics, means that an investigation not predicated on substance but for the political motivations must be dealt with discretely. The county had just finished dealing with Ken Jenne, the federally convicted Sheriff of Broward County – why would the electorate now vote for a man under investigation – having one bad apple follow another? The cynicism of this investigation makes Richard Nixon look like Mickey Rooney at his cherubic best. The intent of the Satz-Miller team to remove the strongest and most empowered candidacy from the race and to use past corruption as a brush to tar Shaan which can only be described as evil, anti-democratic, vicious, but predictable. That they achieved their aim so easily is a measure of how deep the corruption and institutionalized gerrymandering is in the Sunshine State

With surgical precision they removed Shaan from being a major contender – what they also did in this process is Assassinate the Democratic Electoral Process. This was nothing short of an act of internal terror. This attack on the foundation of a republic, a society that prizes above all individual freedoms and democratic societal values cannot be forgiven, forgotten or left unchallenged. The powerful political people of any one generation are not entitled or privileged to destroy the foundations and cornerstones that give the substantive value to a society that boasts of freedom and individual rights for generations to come for the convenience of the day.

The investigation also touched on Shaan's commercial life and activities. It was not enough to derail a candidacy in the public eye without also devastating the economic life line of the candidate – the Shaan Shahrukh Dhanji machine had to be stopped – it supply of money strangulated. Starting in 2007 the tremors in the economy were beginning to show. But these were tremors of adjustment and realignment not of the upcoming collapse that started at the end of the third quarter of 2008. Also during 2007 as Shaan started to prepare for the campaign he started to reduce his daily involvement in his business matters. He wanted more keenly to engage in the campaign to assure its success and victory of his candidacy. He therefore started a process of commercial disengagement and re-alignment. Shaan at the time had a business interest in a real estate based operations that included equity interests in a title company, and a mortgage company. He remained from inception the non-operational equity stakeholder in these. He was the partner that was the rainmaker – bringing in and channeling clients to these enterprises. He also had an interest in retail gas stations and a fuel distribution facility in Monticello, Florida – not far from Tallahassee, the capital of Florida.

Shaan started to make some decisions as to which of his enterprises to continue in that would create the least burden of time – so his focus would remain on the campaign. He decided to step away from the land title business. He continued his interest from a client relations basis only. The mortgage company was otherwise licensed by a colleague and Shaan's father. Only part of the fuel enterprises remained of keen interest – the distribution plant was something he wanted to keep. It was unique and had a licensing agreement to distribute fuel in Florida and Georgia.

The fuel business came along with some interesting characters, including James (Jimmy) G. Villarroel, who was a friend and colleague to Shaan. Jimmy was in the real estate equity lending business. He dealt primarily with private investors and used their money to make loans at high rates of interest – he kept the difference between what he promised his investors and what he loaned the money out for. Jimmy had the technique of what he called the "funky monkey" to "flash the cash", the funds (from his investors) on side deals, close the deals and actually then use the investor funds for the intended transactions. As a matter of operations he always tried to keep an in-house title company to cover his tracks. Jimmy had requested Shaan for the use of his title company in these types of transactions – in polite consideration to the friendship with Jimmy, Shaan had declined his participation in these deals by simply not responding in a timely fashion or indicating overwork in the title agency at the time. Jimmy at a given time was keen to get into the retail fuel business. He through one of his companies agreed to a participation in which Shaan would co-manage operations with him. Jimmy originated the funds for the acquisition of the retail fuel locations and Shaan and he would both be responsible for the loans. Shaan had then structured a plan to do a private placement on the fuel distribution plant – from which he would then also convey to Jimmy a percentage of founder shares. It was the law office of Brenda Hamilton, a noted and reputed securities lawyer that was assisting in the preparation of this structure. This was Shaan's idea to create a financial vehicle that would create distinct operations one that could sell securities to increase its operational capacity and arguably also reduce the burden of debt servicing that was prevalent on the retail side of the fuel business. It was the financial vehicle to alleviate the burdens of debt on the company and the debt liabilities he and Jimmy shared. By 2007 Shaan had signed over his equity interest in the retail operations to Jimmy - this was done in order to preserve the friendship but also because it had become clear Jimmy was interfering with the sale of the retail locations to possible buyers. Shaan had from inception wanted a business model not to collect locations but to buy improve and sell them off while retaining the fuel distribution contracts to these locations. Shaan and Jimmy had both been Co-Managing Partners in the enterprise. However, since there were issues of interference, the lack of Jimmy's availability placed hindrances on making decision in a timely manner – it all placed an unwarranted strain on the business partnership and operations. Jimmy, like so many others in a pressurized society, had a drinking problem. There were times when he simply could not be located. When a meeting would be set up he was generally in a strip club indulging to the fullest extent – not a place where business could be discussed. On one occasion he called Shaan on a Monday morning inquiring how he could dispute an American Express charge in excess of $50, 000 that had been billed out on his Strip Club frenzy over the weekend. Despite trying to be as loyal to friends as he could be and as supportive in any transactional support– Jimmy was not a daily operational partner. However Legal releases and transfer documents were signed in the very midst of the campaign conveying the retail fuel assets to Jimmy. After some weeks Jimmy's demons got to him – feeling a loss of Shaan's business affiliation and possible friendship he reacted with an irrational fit by making contributions to the Lemack campaign under two separate companies that he controlled. Jimmy's offices were located in Hollywood Florida too – Lemacks stomping grounds. Jimmy's assistant Kaney Ratterary and his brother-n-law Bill Knight called Shaan to tell him about Jimmy's actions – in total disbelief.

The question of the fuel distribution operation was another matter. Due to time commitments on the campaign trail the private placement had been put on hold. However, distribution operations had to continue on a daily basis and funds were required to keep an economic life line for Shaan and for him to meet his obligations to his family. Mike Merolle as was later determined to be one of the Agents of Political Cancer, had spent much time in Shaan's operational business environment - the office. He saw the distribution platform with interest and wanted to participate. Shaan saw Merolle at this time as a loyal volunteer in the campaign and someone who might be the right person to get involved as a stock holder and as a daily operations manager. A stock sale for about 7% of the company's shares then held by Shaan was arranged. Agreements and documents were drawn up reviewed and executed. Stock purchase funds then only trickled in from Merrole. Before all the funds for the full sale of stock was transferred to consummate the deal, the stock sale was suspended and resulted in a 100% buy-back from Shaan – dollar for dollar. The process interestingly had taken weeks on the part of Merolle to even commence even the smallest payments. Shaan's buyback action resulted as soon as the duplicity of Merolle's participation in the Lemack camp as orchestrated by the Satz - Miller team had been uncovered. Thereafter, two other gentlemen not associated at all within the political circle came to participate in the distribution facilities operations. Both were sincere and earnest – enthusiastic in their commitment to the business and to Shaan.

The venom of the political attacks that had started under the guise of a legitimate investigation had now permeated into Shaan's commerce world as well. It was the convergence of political attack, it was surreal and a commercial disaster – it was THE PERFECT STORM.

Chapter 8. *Fight or Flight – A time for each*

One of the common failings among honorable people is a failure to appreciate how thoroughly dishonorable some other people can be, and how dangerous it is to trust them. -Thomas Sowell

---

The election for the nomination for Sherriff for the Democratic Party was held August 26, 2008 and not entirely surprisingly to Shaan, he lost. The campaign that had started out strongest with endorsements from the majority of Democratic Party Club presidents and elected officials – with real swelling grassroots supports and novel platform ideas finished last. The investigation was continued to provide some fig-leaf of legitimacy – somehow it had to come to an end and it had to show some wrongdoing. In the world of Florida politics to be accused was to be guilty, and for the investigation to be justified there had to be some charges. So for many reasons – charges had to be lodged. After all of the noise and media coverage had charges not been laid it would become apparent that the investigation was indeed fictitious and entirely designed for political gain, or at least preservation of the status quo and persons and their positions behind the investigation. The investigation took many twist and turns – it went beyond the campaign finance issues and penetrated into Shaan's business world. Every company was investigated, every transaction scrutinized, his bank records subpoenaed, and every colleague, partner and bank relationship questioned. It was a relentless pursuit that devastated commercial relationships with wanton disregard. The appearance of misbehavior in the commercial world is often enough to sow doubt, and if enough mud is thrown, some of it sticks, which was the exact intention.

Interestingly enough the Satz-Miller nominee Rick Lemack, the very good friend of the Special Agent Futch, who was running against Shaan, also lost the election in the primary to one Scott Israel. His loss was by the very margin that would have made the difference in the race – the percentage of votes that went to Shaan cost Lemack his victory in the election. Had Shaan actually been removed from the election that difference of votes would have probably made for a Lemack victory. So Shaan had possibly achieved something even by default.

On one occasion, when the frenzy to find something to pin on Shaan was becoming urgent, it drove the FLDE Agent Futch to Florida's neighboring state of Georgia. There Futch subpoenaed records from attorneys who had previously represented a company Shaan worked for and as a consequence had also represented Shaan. These attorneys pleaded client privilege to the court. FDLE Agent Futch argued that because of the possibilities of some business transactions where wrongdoing may have occurred, this information should be released. One of the attorney's present and a friend of Shaan, Roger Krause reported back that FDLE Agent Futch had described Shaan to the court in Georgia as someone who was "DANGEROUS". The court took the decision that it did not want to hamper an investigation that appeared legitimate in a neighboring state and therefore granted enforcement of the subpoena. Once again the documents obtained through the subpoena led to nothing. The court had effectively granted access on the basis of appearance, that Shaan in the description of an FDLE agent appeared to be "dangerous". And yes, Shaan was dangerous, certainly to those in Florida – the powerful political people that Agent Futch later referred to in his infamous email. The emergence of this email was months later however, too late to have an impact on the election. All that was felt by Shaan at this time was blow after relentless blow from the apparatchiks who knew how to use the system. Ironically this kind of behavior exactly mirrors the way that dissidents are treated in communist countries, they are constantly arrested and harassed by the authorities on the flimsiest of made - up charges.

In no time at all the idea of running for the Sheriff's position had taken a man respected in the community, successful in business and generally well-regarded right through to a disaster beyond contemplation. As these things go so by now the general overall economy was also in a dive. Shaan had been involved in a sizeable real estate project in Jefferson County Florida, begun in 2006, when markets were still booming, was also in a downward spiral. Shaan had the responsibility of dealing with his friends who had also invested in this project. The rippling effect of the Futch investigation touched every one of these persons who were allied with Shaan. A project originally valued in the millions ended in a slow and agonizing demise. Many efforts had been undertaken to sell of the project, but after the sub-prime mortgage crisis and the housing collapse, no buyers could be found. Thanks to friends like Dr. Glen Meyers possible buyers were located in New York – but their review of the project was long and ongoing – and there just wasn't time if the project and the investors involved were going to be saved. Shaan tried to keep the pressure off of his colleagues – there was no point in burdening everyone with the operational detail. Ultimately all these people had participated because the deal made sense and Shaan was going to be the Administrator of the project on behalf of the group. Dealing with the project issues, and the operational management, was his job. His compatriots and two of the main project investors, Howard Gressman and Keith Roberts stayed with him throughout and at least one of them was with him at every meeting. The project was located in Tallahassee, Florida. It was several parcels of land comprising of approximately 45 acres. The ownership at the time was with three siblings who had inherited it from their father. Now they wanted out, as neither of the 3 got along. The possibility of this transaction was brought to Shaan's attention, and he and Keith were the first ones to do an onsite visit. Howard came onto the project almost immediately once the transaction started to take form. The true meaning of the word friend was defined best with Howard - it was and remains a relationship between the two men forged in tested loyalty and trust.

Trying to sell off the project in the erupting mortgage crisis market was going to be prolonged – there were several acres of land and approximately 112 villas – all in contiguous parcels but legally titled in distinct ownerships and parcels. The plan had been to merge the titles and to re-structure the new legal parcel into a homeowner's association. Following on from this the plan was to sell of the villas for a profit rather than retain them as rental units. In what was effectively a crisis situation the only other conventional alternative left was to re-finance. This would have required a whole new valuation. Through a contact of Howard Gressman, a meeting was arranged with a property appraiser who would be willing to undertake a contract to do the valuations for re-finance purposes. The meeting was held at Shaan's home office – which was a ranch home on two and half acres he had acquired specifically for the enjoyment of his children, it provided some natural space in the otherwise growing commercial concrete jungle of South Florida. He had given each child a yearling (young horse), as a way of sealing the idea of space and freedom. Family time was of critical importance and of the greatest enjoyment and happiness. Weekends were about movies, outings, caring for the yearlings, barbeques and family and friends – and at times campouts.

It seemed that Agent Futch had his home under surveillance, and any visitor who seemed out of the ordinary, or not already identified as a close friend or family member, was being questioned after their departure from Shaan's home. This was fishing, something still had to be found in order to make something more than just what had been trumped up in the campaign cycle. But nothing ever was turned up – very simply because there was nothing to turn up. There had simply been no wrongdoing, and no one else except those whom we already know as the Agents of Political Cancer could be counted on to provide the semblance of legitimacy to this now openly acknowledged politically fueled investigation. At the time this was part of that perfect storm – the merging of the political investigation under the guise of something criminal and its effect on the personal and commercial world of Shaan. In a predictable way the new property appraiser who had left the meeting with Shaan and Howard with an agreement to do the valuations was soon visited by Agent Futch. Once again Agent Futch used the color of the law to do the bidding of the powerful political few. A business matter having no connection to anything related to the campaign or the investigation related to the campaign had been impeded and infected. Again predictably nothing more came from the property appraiser, he had clearly taken note of the implicit warning in the "investigation". It seemed that every attempt at the revitalization of Shaan's business in the midst of an economic collapse was being destroyed by the authority of the FDLE through an agent named Futch who was acting beyond the law. Like any whistle-blower Shaan was learning the entire repertoire of the state's ability to blacken and destroy their reputation and thus nullify them.

Shaan was, as they say, between a rock and a hard place, and something different had to be done to achieve a desired result. Every possible commercial exercise would run up against the "investigation" and its ominous tentacles. Anyone visited by the charming Mr. Futch seemed to take fright and disappear faster than drug dealers in a police raid. Shaan was being portrayed basically as a leper and people were keeping their distance. The question was what could be done about it? One avenue was to legally challenge the basis of the investigation, but of course it is very difficult to produce hard evidence of a conspiracy and a lot of money would be needed for this kind of legal action. Richard Rosenbaum's initial estimate of the cost of such legal action was nothing short of 100,000 (USD). At that time such as it had been – servicing this type of a legal budget was untenable.

Given the circumstances there was only one place to go – overseas, basically somewhere where the honourable Mr. Futch wasn't known or acknowledged. New business possibilities could be launched and possible bank or financial relationships could be forged, perhaps even to bring back to Florida. Based on previous contacts and introductions that had accumulated over time but had not previously been entertained, Shaan reached out across the shores of the United States. This kind of business activity, first by emails and phone calls, needs time to assess possibilities that could become probabilities. But time was running out and some kind of undertaking had to be conceived for implementation and action. Florida was now commercially a barren waste land for Shaan – it appeared that so might any other state he might venture into, given what had just happened in the state of Georgia. Business had to be done and successfully to maintain his family and the operations already in existence that were beginning to be stifled with the unwarranted and menacing activities of the Futch investigation. There was also the fact that Shaan needed the income to undertake a necessary legal counter-offensive. It was not just a matter of defending whatever charges might be brought against him – for Shaan it was also a matter of trying to expose a well weaved web of political incest and corruption. That is difficult and expensive work because opposing those that abused a system at will for their personal gain is a seriously uphill task. Shaan's legal counsel Richard

Rosenbaum agreed. It was not just a matter of beating the charges but exposing the truth behind them.

Friends and colleagues like Alex Pappas, whose family were neighbors owning adjacent land to Shaan's Family homestead, Dr. Glenn Meyers and George Saliba suggested that they would provide assistance and support to Shaan to engage in physical trade, especially in the petroleum sector. Based on his prior business history and some connections overseas, specific to the fuel industry, a potential transaction was beginning to materialize. A buyer in the US needing secondary fuel sources for its distribution was identified and engaged with. Overseas contacts in Europe and the Middle East, were prepared to work with Shaan and his group on realistic terms and conditions that were being proposed. The only way to move forward sensibly and clearly was to meet face to face. Looking people in the eye is so important in business, but also to inspect facilities and the product onsite. Then one can sign agreements at the same table and at the same time. Physical presence was fundamental, warranted and required. So Shaan scheduled a flight to Europe (Budapest, Hungry and Bucharest, Romania, respectively) in January of 2009 for a meeting that had been set up for the mid of February, 2009.

The itinerary for departure was from Washington DC on February on the 15th, 2009. It had been over a year and a half since Shaan and the family had taken time off together as had been the customary – with trips to Disney World, a cruise to Mexico's Yucatan Peninsula or a holiday in Europe. Since the campaign and then the endless investigation the ordinary life cycle had become very daunting. The children had gotten a little older and it was decided that it would be a good idea that the family would take a few days in the Washington DC area for the children to experience the MALL (Smithsonian Museums) and the sights in and around Washington – including a visit to Mount Vernon, George Washington's home and Annapolis the US Navy's Academy. Shaan wanted to spend Valentines' day with his wife and family and so the February 14th dinner was at a Greek cuisine restaurant on Connecticut Ave, NW near Dupont Circle.

At the time of this Valentine's dinner (Feb 14, 2009), already known to Shaan a day or two before, the Arrest Warrant had already been issued by the office of the State Attorney Mike Satz and its execution entrusted to one FDLE Special Agent James Futch. The warrant was issued on the eve of February the 10th, its execution was attempted on February 11. The nation saw the ruthless madness of terror on September 11 and here the internal act of terror as perpetrated by those in public trust was being implemented for action in Broward County, Florida on February 11th. The victim of this malodorous internal terror was a fundamental foundation of democracy - the election process. Shaan was simply the fellow that stood up for what he had believed, a clean system void of individual interest where the law is supreme, not usurped by the desire and will of those in temporal positions of authority.

Another intriguing question was why was this man, who was deemed and declared DANGEROUS – by FDLE Agent Futch in a Georgia courtroom not under surveillance prior to and up to the time leading up to the issuance of the warrant or its execution? Ironically surveillance was constant on those unidentified visitors to Shaan's home whilst the investigation was running. Another question is, how is it that the FDLE Agent seemed unaware of the travel itinerary when he had financial and banking records which had been subpoenaed? You don't make travel arrangements without leaving a financial fingerprint, and it was all in the open.

When FDLE Agent James Futch came knocking in glee, Shaan simply was not in the state of Florida. It took a day for Shaan to be reached by his attorney Rosenbaum who in turn had been contacted by FDLE Agent Futch – in search of Shaan's whereabouts. Rosenbaum wanted to know when his client might return. For Shaan the matter of a return was not the question – it was just when? If he returned now this corrupt investigation would be buried- sealed with his arrest, and the real bad guys would get away – yet again. The scales of finance would not swing in his favor and therefore his ability to defend himself would be severely compromised if not totally destroyed, without any means of viable recovery. The complexities of this case was not for a budding attorney from the Public Defender's office – run by Howard Finkelstein. If those powerful political few had to be challenged then the unexpected had to happen as matter of strategy – something that would cause their hand to tip.

Rosenbaum, who had his duty to fulfill in being an officer of the court, as is every attorney, wanted to know when Shaan could surrender. The use of the word "surrender" was an affront to Shaan – a Navy man does not surrender – especially to those that have violated the integrity and principles of everything his Flag stands for. Certainly in wrongdoing there must be accountability – but this was not the case here. This was pretty much High Noon.

In any event a return from Washington to Florida was not going to happen this very day. A return at this point would severely impact and almost undoubtedly torpedo the transaction for which Shaan had already been scheduled to travel for. All business and practical reasons said get to Europe, close the deal – make the money and be back in three to four weeks to take on the fight. With some collateral it might be that by then something might tip in his favor. All strategy and political and practical reasons also suggested doing the unpredictable. To keep to a course as it was, determined by the foe, was not the way to go.

The fight now was not just about the charges filed against Shaan – which were at best laughable. What was unforgiveable to the man, was that this investigation was stinking with a rampant stench of wickedness and corruption. It had with clear intent impacted an election cycle – no investigation is ever to be made public as a matter of policy that can affect an election, save at the threat of human life or loss of property – not remotely the case here. If the electoral process is corrupt then everything else is compromised, and freedom goes to lunch.

The whole nature of the Futch investigation was best described by Daivs Revell Esq., a criminal defense lawyer for the Public Defender's Office in the 2nd Circuit of Florida and a business partner of Shaan's. It was Davis who had sold the family owned fuel distribution facility to Shaan, after Davis's father had passed away. It was a business that Davis's father had started and built up. Shaan bought out most of the shares in the sale and Davis continued to retain a minority percentage. So Davis went from being a seller of a business to becoming a partner with the buyer, Shaan. If anyone could know Shaan from both sides of the fence it was Davis. Davis called after Futch had concluded the interview with him. Davis made two descriptive comments to Shaan – that 'he's just out to get ya, no matter what', and he used the term "witch-hunt".

So the die was cast and the steps now to be taken were pragmatic – certainly right given the overall circumstances – to get to the transaction – to close it and make the money and be back with all haste to battle in court. Shaan got on his flight to Budapest, boarding from Washington's Reagan (National) airport. Like many before him he thought he would be gone for a short time.

He kissed his children, hugged his wife, looked in each of their eyes with endearing love and told them he would see them soon, which he firmly believed. He got through the security gates and took one last look back to the people that made and gave him his purpose in life. With a wave and the gesture of kiss he turned and marched onwards.

Destiny plays many tricks on people, and always hides its face. Shaan little knew it but he was going on an Odyssey.

At the departure gate he called Rosenbaum and informed him he would be back in approximately 3 to 4 weeks – he was off to close the deal so he could have the financial ammunition to make the right legal fight. If FDLE Agent Futch could wait that long great – if not, it was too bad - this course of action as determined by

Shaan was in full force and effect. Unbeknownst to Shaan at the time, for good or bad this journey was going to take much longer that 3 to 4 weeks. The house of political mischief, the Satz –Miller team needed to be exposed and brought down, but, like the Fall of the house of Usher, this was going to be longer, nastier and more complicated than Shaan thought.

Chapter 9. *The Period of Anguish*

"love is the main thing in this earth and against love even death is nothing"
- Rabindranath Tagore

The flight was arduous personally and emotionally. It was an 8 hour flight filled with a tearing heart as though it had been speared into its most inner sanctum of his soul. He had never contemplated the steps he had been compelled to take that had wrenched apart the physical connection shared between his children, wife and himself. All he knew was that it was the love he had for them that empowered him to move forward.

This was about safe-guarding and preserving the political system from corruption – a system that his children (Zayn and Zoya) were going to grow into and had every right to being a part-off, as participant and beneficiaries of a society based on the fundamental democratic societal values. It was also

necessary to generate the appropriate income lines, since business activities had been strangulated in Florida by way of the investigation. On that flight to maintain composure, Shaan took out his dairy notebook and started to write a letter to each of his children – barely being able to read the words he wrote as the eyes were glazed with wetness – he wrote on. The handwriting weakened – but his resolve strengthened. He had a job to do, a mission to accomplish, make the deal, have the financial ammunition to sustain his family and to take the fight on to win – not just to make a plea and walk away as though nothing had happened. That was not the right thing to do and it was far too convenient for those who had taken on to assassinate the electoral process – in the land of the free and home of brave.

Shaan was met at the airport in Budapest by his contact Gabor. Gabor had been an immigrant to Canada – had worked as a Chief Engineer for a municipality in Canada. Upon retiring with a full pension, Gabor returned to his country of birth, Hungry. Gabor's nephew in Canada was a friend on Shaan's favorite uncle on his mother's side of the family. And so weaved the connection of uncles and nephews. Gabor had made contact for the possible international trade that seemed most viable in two key sectors – Petroleum and Infrastructure development in energy and roads. Since Shaan had been involved in the distribution and retail petroleum channels as in Florida – this sector seemed interesting. The proposition was to take on an exclusive and secured relationship to represent a European petroleum interest in the United States. In effect Shaan and his designated company would become the sole and exclusive agent for North America. The European company's platforms were in

Hungry and Romania. Negotiations had been ongoing for some weeks and were successful from a long distance but now physical presence was mandated for a successful consummation. A friend and business ally, Ibrahim Justaniya from Saudi Arabia also in the Petroleum business had provide some of the supportive documents to aid Shaan through the European negotiations. The two would collaborate with resources for the North American venture. It is this transaction that Shaan entrusted to give him back the economic life blood that was so necessary. After a little more than a week in Hungry – it was time to get to Bucharest, Romania to meet the other half of the European team.

The 10 days in Hungry was spent near Lake Balaton. A very picturesque area, a most treasured and frequented holiday location for many Europeans. For all its beauty Shaan's mind remained on the task at hand, and his heart and soul yearned for his wife and children. The meetings were in Budapest and so off Gabor and Shaan went by train – daily. The time required intense concentration while Shaan could only think of the anguish and challenges that faced his wife and children in this period of absence and intentional silence. It pained Shaan not be in contact with his family – but he assessed the necessity of it. If Agent Futch was to come knocking – he did not want his family or friends to be compromised by not answering truthfully or even being in peril of providing evasive answers. After all this was going to be a short deployment of 3-4 weeks and then a return.

The journey to Bucharest was going to be by a night train. Shaan would sleep the night on the train and be ready for meetings starting later the afternoon of his arrival. He had arrived early at the train station in Budapest. After depositing his luggage at the train station in Budapest he we walked across the street from the train station and visited some local stores. He found packets of stamps being sold in one of the stores he had wandered into. Philately was a hobby of Shaan's from childhood and it's a hobby he had inculcated into his two children. So after nearly 10 days of no communication, Shaan decided to buy a memento to post to his children which he did. It was a father's symbolic gesture for his children, that they may know they remained eternally vocal and ever present in his life. Up until now there was no reason to believe Shaan would not be back home in another 3 weeks at the most. He arrived in Bucharest and was ushered away by the local contact Vasile. Here also the relationships were tied through personal and business lines. Vasile provided his fullest commercial resources to Shaan – he knew all too well what this expedition was about, and all that was at stake for Shaan. The initial meetings went on and appeared productive – heading in the direction expected. Initial agreements were drawn up – facilities and resources were inspected and confirmed. All seemed right on course the month was drawing to a close and it so it seemed was also the transaction. All of sudden the momentum came to a shrieking stop - the transaction was in full rupture. In the course of the European side concluding its due diligence – the media frenzy about Shaan and his lack of availability in Florida by local Florida media was all over the internet. The European side simply did not wish to proceed. Although all the commercial resources, points of interest and assets were in place – ready to go, they did not wish to engage. This was despite a show of commitment by Shaan's intent to return and fight the charges. They were also not going to place a moratorium on the matter – it was a fatal commercial and life plan blow. Recovery was going to be an improbability. But Shaan had been in some tight commercial spots before too – he had always managed to pull it off.

Here and now he was in unchartered waters. Something had to be done – but what? The people he relied on most for counsel and advice were not around, and he had with purpose avoided communication for the safety of those he loved and trusted most. However, now that everything seemed to have disappeared into a fateful bottomless pit it was time to initiate contact. If nothing else he could hear himself talk through the options with people he trusted. Shaan undertook to reaching out to the one person he always believed to be his "safe harbor" - it was Amina, his wife. If nothing else he could talk to her if only to hear himself talk his way through the immediate challenge. He counted on her being the confidant.

Amina and Shaan had met on 1995, at the time Amina was exiting from her current marriage of 19 years. Shaan would refer to himself in their relationship after marriage as being her second administration. Holding true to his traditionalism from the Navy which has a CNO (Chief of Naval Operations) Shaan titled Amina affectionately his CDO (Chief of Domestic Operations). She was senior to Shaan by 7 and a half years and had three children from her first marriage. None of it mattered to the two of them – all things were possible, achievable and attainable- their commitment to each other above all was resolute. Like all things of real value in life – those things that really matter and are never lost can only be retained, protected and kept with love and sacrifice – money cannot buy virtue – it can only make things superficially comfortable for a time. Amina was believed to be his love for all time. Time and circumstance would provide the ultimate test.

Time had to be taken to attempt to bring the parties on this European commercial quest back to the table. Shaan extended his stay on Bucharest trying to resuscitate the transaction. Nearly another month passed and the deal was in effect dead. This was another whole month which had passed his time line of expected result and return to America, to the people and things that, made his life whole.

Just as the business side collapsed and all appeared most fatalistic – an emailed popped from Shaan's business partner and friend Howard Gressman. They had not spoken since Shaan had left, and Shaan had with particular notice informed Howard not to contact him until he was contacted. But this email was of critical importance – it was a forward of an email sent to another colleague of Howard and Shaan's. The email had originated from FDLE Special Agent James Futch. In that email Futch wrote ***"some rather powerful political people want to see this man [DHANJI] arrested".*** This was the smoking gun that Shaan always knew existed. This was the crux of the whole matter, he had been targeted as a trouble-maker and the machine was out to remove him, as it had done with many others.

It was the first time that Shaan's suspicions that the investigation was purely political with trumped up baseless charges was admitted to in writing by the Special Agent in charge. The date of this infamous email was April 16. Two months since the arrest was attempted. Frustrations had clearly risen to the surface – FDLE Agent Futch was incapacitated not knowing where Shaan was. Certainly no information was flowing since Shaan himself had orchestrated the lock down. Everything Shaan had done so far was the unconventional to throw the attacker of balance –

clearly doing the unexpected had triggered this incriminating and self-admitting email.

Now was the time to start putting the pieces together. There had been far too many incidents and occurrences during the campaign that had the only purpose of political sabotage that extended beyond even the realm of political filth. The law had been subverted. The state and those that are sworn to act on it behalf had transgressed. The proof was in the very arrogant words placed in writing that admitted that the intent of the investigation was a vehicle of political corruption. The charges themselves as filed against Shaan were no longer the pre-eminent issue for him. The issue of critical dominance was the exposure of those well placed individuals that used their publically entrusted positions and office under color of law to violate the law.

But here was Shaan the accused. Outside of his terrain of familiarity in foreign lands – beyond the embrace of those he loved and that loved him. Most vitally his children and wife. A surrender now would only serve to ultimately clear him - What it would not do is bring those that violated the law to account. The battles still existed – the income was required to stabilize the family at any cost and to expose the truth of the matter now discovered by an admission of the lead investigating officer – FDLE Special Agent Futch.

Again time was needed – to act with a plan. At first Shaan sent of the incriminating email to his attorney Richard Rosenbaum. Richard's initial reaction was "shock". He could not believe that Agent Futch had written that the investigation was politically motivated and instigated. Surrender under these known facts as known now was something most abhorrent to Shaan. Shaan wanted to find a way to invite Federal law enforcement to review of this matter. Very simply there did not seem to be any Federal issues but for the fact that local government had failed by abuse of position of corrupt persons. For a time after this exchange the contact with Richard as would be the case from here on – would remain regularly intermittent.

To remain in Europe made no further economic sense at this time. Shaan wanted time to assess, save on the purse and that could best be done in Asia where the dollar took you further than in Europe. He looked through his passport and found a still valid Visa to India. The choice was made for him by providence. He got on flight to India and landed in the city of his birth Bombay. Here we would try to re-organize lines of commerce and therefore the strategy to action his return to his home in Broward County, Florida.

What he did not know was that fate and destiny had planned a very different journey for him.

Chapter 10. *The Raj (India) and The Kingdom (Thailand)*

"Life is a comedy to those who think, a tragedy to those who feel." — Jean Racine"

Leaving the cold chill of a frozen Balkans Europe in April and flying into the humid hot of Bombay was definitely an immediate climatic shock, not to mention the jet lag. Shaan was once more met at the airport by a local contact, this time by his wife Amina's oldest son through her first marriage – a young man named Shamsuddin. He and Shaan shared a relationship of mutual respect and affection often challenged by Shamshuddin's emotional instabilities that had grown out partially from his parent's divorce. He was a built thin – but solid - all muscle. He was in heart warm and caring – a human being that need just a hug, and to be told he mattered. He had since his parents' divorce been left alone – near abandoned in India – his father had passed away a short 2 years after the divorce of sclerosis of the liver from too much consumption of alcohol. It was a reason the predicated his parent's divorce. Shaan had been most fond of him in particular because of this young man's commitment to his father. No matter what the challenge he never compromised his loyalty to his father, and stayed with him dutifully to the end. Unfortunately life had taken this man on a journey of near emotional abandonment after his father had passed away – being alone he had also become dependent on drugs. Some years later Shamsuddin had made it into the USA. After some time spent in Texas and Florida he had ultimately returned back to India. He was unable to break his dependency on drugs and was unable to adjust to a life-style in North America without some adventure from law enforcement ensuing. From time to time Shaan had sent money to help sustain the boy in India. It was after all what family did for each other, to extend the care and support as and when required in whatever form necessary.

Bombay is where Shaan was born, in many was the place of birth was unfamiliar. He had left when he was 8 years old and only visited twice since then. Not a high frequency destination – twice in over 30 years. It had changed and still in so many ways in memory also remained the same. The name of the city had been official changed to Mumbai but to Shaan it would be and remain Bombay. Coming out of the airport in a sweltering heat and humidity that Shaan was unaccustomed to – Florida was no comparison to the heat of Bombay. He exited the airport terminal into a bustling crowd while Shaan and Shamshuddin both tried to find each other.

From the airport the two journeyed by train to Anand, Gujrat, it is where Shamsuddin had his apartment and where they stayed together for some three weeks. In this time Shamsuddin as had been his practice and continues to be he had once again relapsed into his use of drugs – and the town itself provided no commercial opportunities – except to provide a place of transitory stay. It was another personal conflict with respect to this youngman, but Shaan could do nothing to help at a time when he was sinking himself. He needed to find a firm footing to stabilize, only after which he could extend the hand of support to others. Shaan then returned to Bombay on his own to start once more the process of rebuilding, and in short order he found a residence as a paid house guest with the wonderfully named 'Capt' Arun Sethi. The Captain had been involved in International physical trade of food and consumption product into sub-Saharan Africa. In time the Captain would come to offer much valued guidance in international trade matters.

Shaan still had some lasting generational ties via various friend's families still in Bombay. Some were connections from his early days in primary school at St. Mary's, a highly reputed Catholic school that was set-up by Jesuit priests from the days of the British Raj. Attendance was mandated by family tradition, his father and uncle had also been to the same school, and his grandfather was keen to ensure Shaan would keep in the same pattern. Other connections were of family friends, some with long generational connections. However, all these connections had not been regular or frequent, yet in some respect they provided a valuable starting point. There were two emotional generational ties that bound Shaan in a deep personal way; and it was the memory of his grandfathers, his ancestors. He found himself privileged to be able to call them upon them as spirits to geode him. Even though both were deceased and yet they needed to be visited out of love, resect and memory. So one of the first things Shaan did on his return to Bombay was to go to the respective cemeteries where they had each been laid to rest. These visits would become a matter of routine and each visit would remain distinctively solemn. Sadly there were no immediate descendants from each of the respective sides of the family still in India. Shaan had been the oldest grandchild on both his mother's and father's side of the family and so, in the Indian culture of a successive generations, one could not be in a more valued position. As the oldest he would also be the only grandchild of both these men to have a recognizable remembrance of them. For reasons from the heavens the other younger grandchildren that followed would not have the privilege of time to get to know their grandfather's as Shaan had. He had been graced by the untiring affection and attention of both these men during his early years of his life; and their memories would remain poignant. As a matter of some historical note, his maternal grandfather had established the first auto parts accessories manufacturing company in India, the Press Metal Corporation (PMC). Although the company still existed and its shares were traded on the open stock exchange, no member of the present family was still engaged in any respect in the business. His paternal grandfather was, for his time, in many ways the serial entrepreneur - and his activity along with Shaan's father included the manufacturing of batteries (Regal Battery Corp.) for civilian and military applications. Both families had many "firsts" as accomplishments went in commerce and industry as well as in programs of social development. They were each respectively, men who were captains of industry and society in their time. Shaan retained tremendous adoration for both these men as role models.

But as it is in practical terms the commercial past did not reach into the present in India For the most part real commercial ties and opportunities had to start from zero. After coming into Bombay, it had very quickly become a matter of regimen that Shaan would have dinner at least once a week at the home of Kusum Jagtiani. Kusum was a friend of Shaan's father from a time when they were in their late teens. For various reasons she had never married or had children. Kusum had taken to caring for her ailing father, and life in the traditional Indian sense of marriage and children had simply passed her by. She was a person who had provided much maternal kindness and care – she was like a personal Mother Teresa for Shaan. After a dinner at Kusum's home, Shaan took a stroll through an adjoining neighborhood familiar to him from his childhood memories, nostalgia and images came gushing back to him. The stroll took him through a neighborhood – Umur Park, it was literally an area just across the waves of the Indian Ocean. Across the road from this residential enclave was a park area that fronted the seaside. The park was named after that illustrious philanthropic and industrialists family – the Tata's. You could still hear the sound of the thrashing waves on the rocks and the aroma of the salty sea breeze as it permeated through Umur Park. It all added to the nostalgia of Shaan's walk. Memories of this paternal grandfather taking him to his nursery school in a chauffeured Austin kept creeping back into Shaan's memory. The chauffeured car had been a gift to Shaan's grandfather by the late Aga Khan III, formerly the Secretary General of the League of Nations. Shaan's grandfather had earned the Aga Khan's favor as being his Trustee for affairs in India. Shaan came across Casa Bambino, the nursery where over 40 years earlier he had attended as a young child. Whilst wandering around he happened upon some mechanics working on a vintage car – it was hard to discern the model, but to was a four door convertible in a deep navy blue color. It was relic that was still being maintained that had been left behind from the time of the British Raj. He took a second glance and recognizing the uniqueness of the vehicle approached and started a chat with the person who seemed to be in charge. It turned out that he was also the resident of the Victorian looking house in the yard of which the car was being worked on. He was also the owner of the car, and fittingly he was named Toashar Engineer. Discussion about the car led to him inviting Shaan inside his home, and the two talked over a tea. It was the serendipitous beginning of a new and still lasting friendship.

Toashar was a business man, and entrepreneur, delving into various trades into niche imported luxury oriented products. He became keen to collaborate with Shaan to launch a commercial enterprise. He introduced Shaan to several high end businessmen in the Indian context they were called “high-rollers” One connection made by Toashar to Shaan was with Toony Jatia – whose family are the McDonald Franchisees in India as well as the operators of 5 Star branded hotels such as the Four Seasons. In a short time Toony and Shaan formed what has also become a lasting friendship. They shared home cooked lunches that were couriered to the office daily and after work hours retired to the Cricket Club for networking and meeting other businessmen in the social structure that frequented the private member club scene. It was another practice of social activity left behind by the British Raj. During this time Toony and Shaan formed a mutually convenient business partnership. Toony provided Shaan office space and administrative support as they jointly explored new business trade opportunities – that included supply of sugar into India.

At this time in 2009 India was recovering from a year of poor rainfall, which had had severe effects on the agriculture market, especially the sugarcane crop. It is well known that Indians like sweet foods, and the diminished sugarcane crop meant India needed to import sugar. As the Chinese say in every cloud there is a silver lining and so it would prove for Shaan. Through a series of connections, an introduction was made to a business man Sadhuram Wadwani – the gentlemen owned several sugar mills and whiskey distilleries in India, and he needed sugar for his production. He was a tall man in his 50's with salt pepper hair. A gentleman by any standard and a seasoned businessman. He had the balance of kindness and shrewdness dispensing each aspect of his character as warranted by situation and circumstance. Wadwani's group included a joint venture partner by the name of Vinesh Chandanvania, a newcomer to the physical commodity trade business. For Chandanvania being affiliated in a deal with Wadwani was a ticket to the big game. The two men had engaged in an agreement to acquire several thousands of tons of sugar from Thailand on a monthly basis but required assistance and support for the underwriting and structuring of the transaction. Shaan's business background and legal training made him the logical selection and conveniently present choice for Wadwani and his group.

A services agreement was entered into where a success fee would be charged by Shaan for himself and his partner Toony Jatia – which was payable at lift on a monthly basis for a period of twelve months for the consultation. In the interim a monthly service fee would also be paid to Shaan for the ongoing consultation onsite as "boots on the ground". This arrangement provided the necessary money essentially required for his children and Amina – so Shaan started monthly transfers in support of this immediate need and objective. The underwriting of the deal required terms and conditions and a Letter of Credit in conformity with the purchase and sales agreement, an onsite visit and meetings with the product supplier and seller. So seven months after he had last seen his adoring children, here he was in September of 2009 and it seemed finally a real deal was in the making that would provide enough financial capital to secure the family and take on the important legal battle. It had been long enough, and Shaan wanted to be back. His daughter Zoya is his Princess whom Shaan calls his Precious and his son Zayn who was always to Shaan his "Number 1" they had both remained the bravest and noblest of characters, no Father could boast more dedicated and loyal children to be proud of. They too needed and craved for their Father just as he wanted a 100 fold more to be with them too. Amina had remained seemingly loyal, albeit frequency of communication was breaking down. Daily attempts on Skype calls continued by Shaan as well as emails that were ignored or answered as and when. In a short term the income stream being generated was to become the only basis for any relationship, communication and a leverage for continued and uninterrupted contact between the father and children. At the time, it seemed finally the family might be in one place again in a matter of a few short weeks, and things might fall into place on all fronts for the best.

In September 2009, Wadwani, Chandanvania, an administrative aid from Wadwani's organization and Shaan boarded a flight from Bombay to Bangkok, the Kingdom of Thailand, and the land of the Orchid. On arrival in Bangkok they went immediately to check in at the 4 Star hotel AMARI on New Petchburi Road, one of the primary commercial avenues in Bangkok. That evening at the hotel the sugar supplier came to meet with them all, his name was Sir Anam Islam. He was a UK national with Bangladeshi roots. He was a balding dark skinned, slightly pudgy fellow, always with a grin – which was oddly sinister. His English in speech as enunciated was reflective also in his writing – typical for an immigrant's use of the language. Despite his claims of academic accomplishments (from being a medically trained doctor to now being in the world of business) he simply did not know the difference between the words and use of "patience" and "patients". Little things that would raise the flag of concern for a critical listener. He had a convincing story of the title of "Sir" being awarded to him by the British Crown for his works in philanthropy

– a boastful self-serving assertion that strangely was never followed by any specifics of acts or deeds. Sometime later it was discovered that the "Sir" was not a title but rather a legal name change he had gone through to make his first name "Sir". At the time of the first meeting this was not known. Sir Anam Islam's story at the first meeting continued by his self-professing that his business enterprises included an agricultural interest with Thai sugar suppliers, specifically with a fellow with some political influence named Somsak. The pitch seemed all very impressive for the Indian businessmen. Strangely the sub-continental culture still seemed to be in awe of the British crown's self-empowering indulgence to convey titles – that were in all reality to an American like Shaan nothing more than regalia bearing no commercial value. If it came down to titles alone to do a business deal, Shaan had a few of them himself – but he know far too well what was needed was not showmanship but results. Shaan simply wanted to know there was product and the terms and conditions could be fulfilled by the supplier – with or without the title of "Sir". A time was set-up for a warehouse visit to confirm the existence of product, a simple but important step in any transaction. The morning of the site visit unfortunately Wadwani slipped and fell in the bathtub of his hotel room and had to be taken to the hospital. This was an omen for everything else that was to follow.

Wadwani's administrative aid accompanied him to the hospital. Chandavania and Shaan proceeded to the port warehouse for inspection. They were taken by Sir Anam Islam and Somasak in a large chauffeured gold coloured Toyota SUV. They were accompanied by two other Thai staffers of Somsak – all looking very official as Somsaks personal security detachment. Somsak himself had a good understanding of the English language but was uncomfortable speaking it. He generally kept silent – listening mostly unless one of his guards at his request also did some translating for him. He was heavy set in body structure and wore thin rimmed spectacles. His personal security guards shrouded their eyes with dark sunglasses, loose untucked shirts, and always with a seeming inadvertent quick flash of a semi-automatic side holstered 9mm Glock, all to give them that look. It also seemed a bit too Hollywood but whether the firing pin was still in the weapon – loaded or not is something Shaan did not want to find out. They entered the port warehouse area on a Sunday – and after a cursory security checkpoint where Somsak flashed an official looking ID and his vehicle was given the wave through.

At the warehouse there seemed to be an inspection of the product underway by SGS representatives and a conveyor belt loading product on to a vessel for presumably a shipment. Chandanvania walked over to the conveyor belt – saw some white powder crystals and stuck his finger into the crystal and then proceeded to taste it – it was sweet and it was sugar. This all seemed to be in order.

Shaan started to walk over to a SGS inspector and wanted to chat to try and assess the product and ownership beyond the finger lick test of off a conveyer belt. As soon as Shaan's intention was noted, Sir Anam Islam made the intercept and stated that no contact should be made with the SGS inspectors while they were screening the product for loading. Shaan not wanting to cause a disruption at this point, obliged. After all he intended to later ask for verified documents confirming the ownership and the ability to sell the product contracted for purchase with his client. He also wanted to confirm the banking and commercial offices of the seller's, Sir Anam Islam, Somsak and their company Commodities Trading International. For the time being enough had been done for a Sunday, and Chandanvaia wanted to get back hurriedly to check on Wadwani at the hospital. Obviously Chandanvaia was obliged to check to see how the senior partner with the majority of the funding of the deal was doing from his slip and fall – in fact Wadwani unfortunately had a fracture in his forearm.

Due to the unexpected medical condition that had developed the trip to Bangkok was cut short – Wadwani and Chandanvania returned to Bombay. The Administrative aid and Shaan remained behind to carry out tasks, finalise the deal and such instructions as transmitted on behalf of Wadwani and his group. Shaan had shared his observations back in Bombay with the veteran physical trader 'Capt' Arun Sethi. There were matters of some real concern – Why a visit to a port facility and warehouse on a Sunday – when it should have happened during a work day. Why was contact by presumably SGS inspectors not permitted, and was it customary for SGS to be working on a Sunday in Thailand?

Shaan was of course concerned of the possibility of it being a "con job". There were too many red flags and the international trade arena was full of alleged suppliers and buyers, each one trying to sell or trade a product they may not have – just enough to take on a deposit and make a run for it. Some research on the NET should how some of these perpetrators in the commodity industry operated.

Here was one recent classic example from www.koalaglobal.com. The headline was PAYMENT WHEN there was NO PRODUCT. It went on to say that "On 25th July 1991, a Bulgarian buyer paid US$3.8 million for 13,100 tonnes of Brazilian sugar by letter of credit. The payment was released by International banks on the basis of the usual documents which proved that the sugar was loaded on 17th July in the port of Santos on the m.v. Giovanna bound for Varna, Bulgaria."

Neither the ship nor the sugar existed and the criminals have never been brought to justice.

Or another example - In August 1992 a Paris bank released US$2.89 million under a letter of credit on the basis of documents stating that 10,000 tonnes of white refined sugar had been loaded on the m.v. Vladimir Ilyich in Panama, bound for Kalingrad, Russia.

The documents were forgeries and the money has never been recovered.

As we know diamonds can be faked and old master paintings can be forged, but commodities are more easily measured and tested and are rarely of sufficient value to attract forgers. With commodities however the fraudulent transaction is almost invariably based on a consignment which does not physically exist. Although somewhat surprising at first glance, this potential arises because bureaucracies everywhere have engendered a belief in the authority of paperwork. Just as worthless paper money is accepted as actually having value, so pieces of paper are accepted as having real value, so pieces of paper are accepted as proof that a consignment of a specific commodity exists. The ordinary man does not go to his central bank to check his wealth in gold - he relies on a statement of account on a bit of paper. By the same token, commodity documentation is taken on trust. It is only necessary to forge documents showing the existence of a consignment and to find someone to buy it.

The victims of fraud are almost always attracted by the expectations of exceptional profit. They succumb more to their own greed than anything else. A deal which is too good to be true probably isn't true - yet people around the world queue up every day for all manner of schemes which could not logically be genuine. (Think about Bernie Madoff and his 20% endless payments Ponzi scheme) Commodities are openly traded on all the world's major commodity exchanges and their prices are fairly exactly established. There are also several long-standing international commodity traders of the highest repute. Offers to sell commodities at less than the ruling market price makes no commercial sense - unless the real motive is fraud. This has been a standard ploy since time immemorial: to make the victim believe that he has access to a phenomenal deal; so good that he wants to keep it secret. This greed enables the fraudulent seller to conceal detailed information about the origins and location of the commodity. The buyer thinks he is on to something no-one else knows about, which will make him a quick profit, and doesn't care too much about the origins of the commodity or why it is cheap, so long as it is genuine - and the documents appear to protect him on this point. To allay suspicions a fraudulent seller will often offer various assurances which seem to give protection, or at least to vindicate his character. He may lodge a performance bond equal to say, 2% of the value. He is then risking 2% in the hands of an honest buyer in order to swindle him of the remaining 98%. He may provide various attestations from banks as to his financial worth (of no real legal value or protection). He may offer to supply secret information about the exact location and origins of the commodity in return for, say, a 10% part payment, either as a means of consolidating the deal or simply to the abscond with the part payment. The provision of unnecessary quasi-official documentation is another tactic; any bit of paper which seems to confirm the existence of the commodity provides further re-assurance. Victims are usually surprised and even outraged when they discover that the international banking system provides absolutely no protection against payments made on the basis of fraudulent documents. They fail to understand the rules of international payments systems and the division of responsibility between themselves and the banking system. To say may the buyer beware seems almost anodyne. It is always the psychological greed of the buyer that leads them to see what they want to see.

The common commodity fraud utilizes the normal international trading practice of payment via irrevocable letter of credit. The buyer first arranges for his bank to issue a letter of credit. This is a legal undertaking by the bank, not the buyer, to make payment when certain specified documentation is provided which "proves" the commodity exists and is in transit to the buyer or at some agreed location - documents the fraudster of course intends to forge. Note that it is the bank which gives the undertaking, albeit at the buyer's expense. The letter of credit is also irrevocable so the buyer is now entirely in the hands of his bank and the seller. Any alteration to the terms of a letter of credit must be agreed by both parties, so that the buyer is powerless even if he becomes suspicious. The crucial point is that banks deal solely in documents, not commodities. They are protected by international banking rules (the Uniform Customs and Practice for Documentary Credits) which stipulate that a bank must honor a letter of credit if the specified documents are presented and appear to be correct in relevant details. They have neither the obligation nor the incentive to question the documents; only that they apparently accord with those specified and there is nothing which suggests forgery. In point of fact banks have more incentive to detect forged currency notes or cheques, where they stand to lose themselves. It is up to the buyer to make independent checks. For example, in the case of the US$3.8 Million fraud described above, it would have been simple to establish with Lloyds Register of Shipping that the m.v. Giovanna was nowhere near the Brazilian port of Santos in July 1991. It had been renamed the m.v. Styliani in 1983 and broken up for scrap in Pakistan in 1984.

It seemed “Sir” Anam Islam was on a similar track, albeit with some new variations. It became more obvious as his game plan unfolded and it was not too long before it did.

Shaan requested from Sir Anam Islam proof of supply or allocation in his company name, the company's registration documents and at the least a warehouse receipt showing that in fact there was product titled to Sir Anam Islam and his company for immediate sale, and that the appropriate export licenses were also in place.

Nothing that Sir Anam Islam provided could be verified - it was not for lack of paperwork and documentation – it was just that none of it checked out. All rational and reasonable common sense suggested a termination and a pull back. Sensibility and common sense in this deal took a back seat to the "finger licking test" Chandanvania had done at his port warehouse visit on that fateful morning of Wadwani's slip and fall. That "finger-licking test" was all that was required for the principals of the group to engage full steam ahead into the deal. Greed often overrules good sense in commerce and 'caveat emptor' is often forgotten.

Shaan went to the office address on Sir Anam Islam's company letterhead and found the address lead to a back ally in Bangkok with no street number to attach to the address. A check with the official company registration office showed the company had been formed only within the month and a visit to the bank confirmed the account was set up barely a week prior to the group's arrival in Bangkok. The product allocation document was a self-serving letter between two companies sharing common and controlling shareholders. It was a near perfect "con" so long as one did not seriously start investigating and scrutinizing the documents and the story being presented. Shaan reported these findings back to Bombay. He too wanted the deal to be completed successfully but was not going to ignore these alarm bells and not at least suggest a halt or more time to assess the risks. The obvious goal was to protect the client – the Wadwani Group. If this deal was not real then another would come along and Shaan saw himself as the vanguard that would protect this group's interest – and in doing so secure a long time client with mutual loyalties. But it seemed the dire need for the Bombay people to have product for their four factories, which were at near standstill for lack of raw material, meant that for them sugar could not wait any longer. Warnings were not being heeded.

Despite a written email strongly recommending a pullout or at least a delay for further verification from Shaan the instructions that followed from Bombay were to engage with all haste. It was to become apparent that Asian business was not based on the value of documents and contracts but rather on conversation, presentation, the "finger licking test" and some notion of 'belief', which for Shaan belonged in a church or temple not in a business deal. The sweetness of the deal was proving too alluring.

Sir Anam Islam had initially agreed to and assented to a 100% Letter of Credit as means of payment. After Wadwani had left he announced that he needed about 10% of the payment in advance by Telex Transfer – in effect 10% cash up front or he could not secure the product for Wadwani as he had other buyers waiting who wanted to buy his product just as quickly. He claimed he extended the courtesy of a letter of credit to Wadwani as he wanted to build a longer term relationships with a regular buyer. Nonetheless he now needed the 10% in advance to make the first deal happen. To anyone inside or outside of this transaction, with any knowledge of the jungle of the business world, the smell of a confidence game was as strong as a hot curry. The Buyer was desperate for the product and so the seller was modifying the arrangements for a cash advance, and promising the world. It was a classic business style con, a bushwhacking of near perfect design.

The amount of the first transfer was a not insignificant 700,000 USD. Zarifa Rizvi who was organizing the financial instruments and payments for this deal for the Wadwani Group arranged a transfer of 400,000 USD directly to Sir Anam Islam's company, Commodities Trading International. The balance of 300,000 USD was then transferred to Shaan's account, which he had set-up at the request of Rizvi. She had explained that the full 700,000 USD could not be wired directly due to some banking regulation in India. It made no sense to an American why there would be any restrictions on the amount of a transfer for a legitimate business deal. Clearly, although quite a substantial amount, it was not such a large amount within the international trade business. Not to hold up the matter, and despite his reservations, Shaan set-up the account. He also stressed that it wouldn't be prudent to transfer just funds into Sir Anam Islam directly until verification could be properly concluded – that it might be sufficient to show the funds were real and ready to transfer pending verification of the product deliverability. It seemed that the Bombay group trusted with the finance operations had greater reliance, to their total detriment, on the unknown personage of Sir Anam Islam more than their underwriter and representative for the Wadwani group on the ground. Shaan had raised too many issues of concern and was perhaps being seen as difficult. The wire to Shaan's account was sent on the eve of the day before Rizvi arrived in Bangkok, so that she could go with Shaan to his bank to ensure the balance of all the funds were in effect transferred to Sir Anam Islam and or his company. The expectation was that once this was done the sugar would be delivered and Wadwani's facilities would be back in full production. Nothing could be easier and money was waiting to be made, the hook had been taken and the fish was about to be played.

Rizvi had intended to stay in Bangkok for a week to monitor the completion of the transaction and then return to Bombay. In fact she stayed on for nearly 3 weeks, only returning because of the demand of family needs back in India. She had realized, just as Shaan had, that something was not correct with the Sir Anam Islam business pitch. There were supposed issues being created in relation to the letter of credit that were simply being conjured up as Shaan saw it. When there are delays in the delivery of a contract, or failure to perform by either side, it is a default and whatever assets have been pledged such as a deposit are generally forfeit. This was Shaan's main concern and it soon came to be realized as a legitimate one, spurious claims in relation to the letter of credit were simply a smoke-screen for fraud. Rizvi too became alarmed but it was too late the funds had all been transferred, and the loss was imminent. Only after the Bombay buyers began to realize the possible impending disaster was Shaan re-consulted on what, if anything, could be done to mitigate if not eradicate the loss. So Shaan set-up a meeting with Sir Anam Islam and Rizvi prior to her departure at the Amari Hotel which was becoming a temporal residence. The hotel was a hub for visiting tour groups, overnight airline crews and businessmen. Always bustling with activity with hotel staffers well positioned to greet and assist guests – always with kind greetings in Thai (Sawadi Kharp). It was an extremely modernized and sprawling facility.

After pleasantries Shaan informed Sir Anam Islam that the deal needed to be called off and the funds returned. Shaan knew well that this would not happen but he needed a position to start negotiations from. After all once money has been sent – it rarely does a u turn and comes back, and in particular when the integrity of the principal on the other side of the fence is already being questioned. After a short discussion period of about 45 minutes it was agreed that Sir Anam Islam would not cancel the deal nor return the funds but provide a check for 23 million Baht (equal to the amount of the 700,000 USD transfer) and that this would be his guarantee that if the shipment did not happen this cheque could be used for a return of the funds. This was not the best guarantee in the world but it was better than nothing. And as the good con man that Sir Anam Islam was, he would always say yes in order to buy the time to make his effective getaway.

What Shaan had predicted in September was what eventuated in March. After the six months of prevarication and promise there was no shipment and there was no Sir Anam Islam. Despite emails and communications continuing almost to the last, nothing actually happened. Every last attempt was made to keep the promise of the product being delivered and to avoid the check of 23 million baht from having to be negotiated. With a heavy heart Shaan took the check to his bank on day 179 and deposited it – knowing it was going to be dishonored. It had to be done to preserve their rights under the law to pursue criminal prosecution.

During this six months Shaan had continued to work for and represent the Wadwani group's interest, and he did this by remaining in Thailand. He found alternative sugar suppliers who could actually deliver. The Wadwani group eventually got moving despite Sir Anam Islam and his bag of tricks. Payment for Shaan's services continued with monthly remuneration reaching Amina and his kids back in Florida, albeit under modified terms since the debacle of Sir Aman Islam. Shaan simply needed enough to keep himself going from day to day and hopefully find a deal that didn't involve scamsters. This was like trying to find an honest politician in Florida.

Strangely throughout this ordeal for Shaan the situation in Bangkok the capital of Thailand, reflected the immense political discord that was also fermenting throughout Thai society, as though things weren't already difficult enough. This was all the result of what came to be called the Red Shirt protest. "Red" because that was the color of the shirt worn by the supporters of the democratically elected Prime Minister Thaksin Shinawatra who had been removed in a military coup in 2006. The protests escalated into prolonged violent confrontations between the protesters and the military, and attempts to negotiate a ceasefire failed. More than 80 civilians and 6 soldiers were killed, and more than

2,100 injured by the time the military successfully cracked down on the protesters on 19 May 2010. Oddly the current Prime Minister at the time had his residence on the very same street as the twenty room hotel that Shaan was staying in. Very frequently the protesting marchers would come down the street, and Shaan was witnessing first hand a major socio-political protest, The Red Shirts had managed to barricade themselves in at a major intersection of the commercial district in Bangkok – an area that Shaan traversed daily. This section of the city was blocked by the Red Shirts with tires and bamboo, while the opposite side of this major intersection was manned as a secure perimeter with riot and crowd control police and the military. Before it all ended after almost 90 days in May of 2010 under a military order and a violent action of a deployed combined force of 50,000 men the largest shopping mall in Bangkok had been set ablaze and devastated. The government of Prime Minster Abhisit Vejjajiva which had taken office in December 2008 was just about preserved. Despite this very volatile situation and the difficult problems for Shaan it was an oddly fitting backdrop for what his objectives were – to persevere regardless of the otherwise stormy situations.

Many days and months had passed in Budapest, Bucharest, Bombay and Bangkok, sometimes walking the streets, sometimes drinking to forget some of the difficulties. Shaan marched more in these several months than he ever had on the campaign trail or in uniform – or so it felt. His love of his children kept him moving forward, in the determination of knowing his convictions were right. The pain of separation somehow also gave him further resolve. He held on to that inner pain – it was in a way the fuel he needed to keep moving to get to the intended goal. The ultimate aim was the exposure of the truth that had driven him so far from home and out of reach of the three most important people in his life, his children and wife. The process of life, the destiny, this journey now undertaken was necessary if he was ever going to challenge and halt the progress of the internal terror of those "powerful political people" who had set out to destroy him. Ideals are difficult to live by and to think about the society and the way of life that he wanted to protect for his children without the violation of the "powerful political people" was a hard road to furrow. Shaan's America was one that lived under the law, with equality to all, not to be governed by those in temporary positions of power, and the system had to preserve eternally. In the middle of his travails across the globe it was often hard to hang onto these ideals.

Finally, Shaan took the dishonored check, all supporting documents and a letter of authority from the Wadwani group and filed a police complaint against Sir Anam Islam, Somsak and their company Commodities Trading International. The process got all the way up to a meeting with the Central criminal investigation bureau for Thailand – and there it rested. Somsak had enough political cover at the time and Sir Anam Islam had flown the coup to his home in Cheshire, England. For the moment this matter had come to a halt, once more the law could be used and abused by those with the right connections. About two years later Somask would be indicted for being the kingpin of the sugar scams in Thailand - but that was all that would happen -the indictment – millions were scammed and there was no restitution for anyone. So much for the criminal enforcement of white collar international trade scams in Thailand, and let the buyer beware. Sadly this was the way many places in Asia worked. Buddha's philosophy of kindness and integrity in the everyday social world was mixed with the double edged sword of expediency for the easy slice and dice in doing business with foreigners.

While wandering in Bangkok, Shaan had stepped into a restaurant lounge on a Sunday afternoon – the Penalty Box on Sukumwit Soi. Intrigued by the name but never having been there before he stepped in – but it was empty apart from the waiters. Only the endless honking of the cars and the street noise infiltrated this otherwise strangcly empty sports restaurant and lounge. He found a place to sit by the open arches next to the sidewalk, and at the table he choose to his delight he found a folded English newspaper– there was something to read while he could sip the coffee he had just ordered. A few minutes later in walked another

European fellow and took a table also along the sidewalk. He sat down and ordered a beer and after being served asked Shaan if he could borrow the newspaper. Shaan replied – “by all means, it’s not my paper either – I just found it here”. They struck up a conversation as one would in a strange place with a fellow English speaker, after a few minutes of an exchange the two men were now seated at the same table. The man turned out to be one Jay Boccia, a film producer and director. He was of Italian descent having spent many years in South Africa, and was now spending time between Hollywood, California and Bangkok, for films he was shooting. That Sunday encounter and chance meeting would be the commencement of a friendship based on shared values and interests – loyalty, friendship, confidentiality, trust, and belief in democratic values and politics. Sometimes Kharma plays a beneficent role in the affairs of men.

Jay provided the sense of present brotherhood that had been missing since Shaan’s exile journey had started. On one occasion Jay simply pointed out to Shaan that the charges in Broward County, Florida are put into perspective when you think of how diminutive Broward County is to Florida – and Florida to the USA – and even the USA to the Americas and then in comparison to the world. He argued that with perseverance and tenacity Shaan would overcome and indeed prevail through upholding right over the wrong done him. Also through Jay, Shaan met Fotinin Loumbardia, a former diplomat with the Greek Embassy in Thailand, who had stayed on and set up a garment manufacturing enterprise in Thailand for customers in Europe. With that entrepreneurial spirit that many Greeks have she also ran the first, and at the time, the only Greek restaurant in Bangkok. She was keen to expand her business activities and was interested in the physical trade/commodities business and on that basis she and Shaan formed an association. Interestingly, Shaan was already thinking about this and had started to create an Indo-Thai network for commerce. The network would umbrella Toony Jatia in India and Fotini Loumbardia in Thailand as the key principals in the two respective venues. The trade objective was to establish a reliable and credible supply channel of food items. Business practices were compromising – the culture of business practice seemed more on handshakes that often lacked honor and integrity and less on the reliance of agreements and contracts – something Shaan was accustomed too. It proved fruitful for a time and as money got made, he made sure funds were sent across to Florida for Amina and the kids. It was and remained a difficult time for the family – Amina and the Kids being the very essence of Shaan's universe. Still the deal necessary to bring in a large enough income stream necessary for sustaining the family and the legal fight back in Florida had not materialized.

Shaan had committed to seeing the children and Amina and even asked Amina to consider preparing for a flight for a short 2 week visit over school holidays was curtly brushed aside. It seemed personal commitments and convictions Shaan had believed unwavering had indeed latent fractures. Shaan was now feeling the absolute pangs of abandonment, he had never thought this relationship would ever fall to these depths. He was indeed the exile doomed to wander forever.

George Saliba the friend from South Florida who had contacts in the Americas and Europe also provided resources for possible business. He had kept trying to connect with Shaan after he had left, but was only able to re-establish communication with Shaan in Thailand. More than business possibilities, George brought the much needed emotional familiarity of someone from Florida and Shaan's life from back home. After nearly 9 months in Thailand, six of which were on behalf of the Wadwani group, Shaan had realized that remaining in Asia was not going to make the kind of transaction he was looking for in order to produce the wherewithal for his return to the USA. The business culture in this part of the world was not going to be conducive to the serious fast actioning and substantive business that Shaan was accustomed to and needed.

After conversations with Jay and Fotini, it was decided that the best course of action would be a return to Europe, specifically London, which was the major commerce hub and where language would not be a hindrance. It was also a venue where there had been some tangible and useful connections – personally and professionally. London however is expensive and Shaan had enough to hold him up for about a month. In that time he would have to swim – sinking was not an option. At the same to remain under the existing conditions in Asia was to be dead in the water. This was a new venture times ten and, of course, every step was difficult.

Jay offered up some connections, so did Ibrahim Justaniya from Saudi Arabia, Shaan's supportive college from the original transaction that brought Shaan to Budapest to begin with. Some other connections were offered from various contacts, including Kusum Jagtiani, who had a sister and some close friends in London. There was then a potential support system in place, albeit untested and unproven. Being there, finding contacts and unfettered resolve would do the rest. From proceeds of a trade deal that he had done with Fotini, Shaan purchased his tickets for London, and his good friend Jay would follow a day or two later and would also be in London for a week on other business.

Shaan spent the next week to 10 days getting ready for departure. Relationships in business and friendships had been formed in these nine months – there were farewell meetings, and dinners. On several occasions while in Bangkok, Shaan had been invited to the Perdomo Club (a member's only private cigar club and lounge) by an American Expat and founder of the Club, Hillman Lenz and his colleague at the Club, James With who was also professionally engaged in the film and entertainment business. James had been involved in the film making of movies such as the Patriot and Independence Day. Of late he was more disposed to engaging in the technological developments that had occurred in filmography as scene in the movie AVATAR. He was also keen to promote the film and entertainment industry in South East Asia, and so he had made his new residence in the region, specifically Bangkok. Other colleagues like Mark Duchiene who was Dutch but had spent over 25 years in Thailand and also involved in the commodities industry. It was always good to be with Mark in a business meeting with other Thais, because of his language skills. He looked European and no one expected him to understand the Thai language. We managed to learn more by the appearance of an overall idea that we were unfamiliar with the language – until Mark spoke out in Thai. Not only could he understand it, he would write and speak in Thai. Mark spent the last afternoon with Shaan and went along to the airport to wish him well and safe journey. Mark had actually hosted Shaan with some other friends at a farewell dinner of fondue a night or so before departure. There were many more people but these few people mentioned were the key and daily supporters and friends in Shaan's journey thus far. They had given Shaan sincere friendship and company – it helped keep a clear frame of thought in what had become a time of personal challenges not just ones predicated by the finances of the moment.

Shaan boarded the evening flight from Bangkok for an early morning arrival at Heathrow – London. Rather like the Pilgrim in Bunyan's classic the Pilgrim's Progress Shaan set out each time ready for the new battles ahead, and determined to stick to the path that would lead him to the promised land, or at least to the sunny streets of Florida.

Chapter 11. *Big Ben – Tolled.*

"Hard is trying to rebuild yourself, piece by piece, with no instruction book, and no clue as to where all the important bits are supposed to go."

— Nick Hornby, *A Long Way Down*

Every journey starts with one small step, but all journeys are different, and some are more difficult than others. Shaan's latest journey started with his arrival in London. His arrival was in the early morning at London's Heathrow, and the UK Border Officer looked into Shaan's passport and commented, "I don't know how your guys do it". He had seen lots of travel stamps in Shaan's passport from several years of travel – even from before this current trek, which had had begun from about a year and a half ago. He had guessed Shaan was some type of businessman on the international scene or more likely someone on the government payroll – which was pretty far from the reality at hand. He gave Shaan a smile with a welcome stamp in the passport to enter the UK.

The rebuilding was about to start again.

From the airport it was off to a Hotel near the Earl's Court tube station, not far from where the Poetry society was housed, and where there was the so-called battle of Earls court in the 1770's between the radical poets and the old guard, which the radicals lost! This particular bit of arcane history was completely lost on Shaan as the hotel was found and reservations made online. The hotel was the typical 3 star hotel in West London, with all its charms and drawbacks. It was an old and large Victorian or Edwardian style building that had been not particularly well converted into a hotel. Like so many hotels now run by those with Asian or Sub-Continental roots, this hotel simply failed in standards in maintenance and repair. The rather shabby room was the size of a walk in closet Shaan was accustomed to by American standards. It was a far cry from the ensuite Shaan had been in just a year before the campaign, when he and Amina had taken his children Zayn and Zoya for their second family holiday to Europe. At that time the stay had been at the Marrlott at Grosvenor Square. This was once a stately apartment building overlooking Hyde Park and Marble Arch, and is now one of the leading luxury hotels in London.

Being back in London was difficult and nostalgic for many reasons. Life had taken its twist and turns in every aspect, many not even conceivable. When leaving India as a young boy of 8, Shaan and the family had lived in London for nearly six months before eventually leaving for North America. Memories about Hyde Park, walking in Regents Park, the tubes, Selfridges and Duke Street that lead up to it were some of the strongest memories that had stayed. He never forgot Duke Street. The 68 Duke Street address is where Shaan's paternal Uncle had a clothing store selling leather coats – that was back in 1975. Since then this Uncle too had relocated to the United States, another one to make the USA a successful immigrant story.

Shaan had also more recently been through the UK when he was sent there during his time with the US Navy. So in many ways at least London was familiar territory, but harder than ever, as everyone knows London just gets more and more expensive. He had arrived on a Saturday morning and after checking in the first order of business was to get a local SIM card and get communications up and running. He had a quite long list of people and contacts that had been provided that he needed to start reaching out too. Even if it was a Saturday – there were some contacts that were expecting him – and time was never treated as a luxury by Shaan. He had always agreed we can make more of everything – except time, and so he got his communications started.

Meanwhile back in Florida his family were probably having a quite tricky time. When Shaan checked by email and Skype with Amina – and inquired about the children he found that what had once been a right of practice now started to became a privilege – getting consent to speak to his children. Clearly some things were changing, and none of it made any sense. Whenever he spoke to his kids they wanted just as badly to speak to him – love and lots of adoration flowed through the conversation. His son and daughter would compete with each other over who had more to share with Dad – these moments where embellished by father and both children. Zayn and Zoya remained their father's most stalwart supporters. No doubt the communication retained much of the emotional strength relationships were challenged by and needed badly. Despite this, these were difficult times however.

Back in the slightly dispiriting hotel in west London Shaan was back at work, the calls on Saturday went out to Ahmed Wani, introduced to Shaan by his Saudi colleague and friend Ibrahim Justaniiya. Wani and Shaan had made contact while Shaan was still in Bangkok, trying to make sugar into a sweet deal. Someone else that was referred to Shaan was Hitish Shah, who was also a physical commodities trader. Both these people confirmed meeting times on Monday and Tuesday, respectively. Once again things were on the move with a quick start. Also Jay was flying in the next day and they would also meet along with some other friends of Jay's in London over dinner. Whilst London is good fun however it is still prohibitively expensive, and Shaan's hotel was like a bloodsucker. Something had to be done.

Meanwhile Shaan was out meeting the people, and he met Hitish Shah aboard the rather exotic St Katherine, it had been Queen Victoria's former river yacht, and apparently she did not use it very often. Now it had been converted into a floating hospitality platform – a private club – the Yacht London. During several meetings at the club, Shaan had come into the contact with the Clubs founder, Prince Muzaffar Siddique Khan – "Poncho" to his friends. Poncho was a tall and stately looking figure – refined in speech and demeanor with a well groomed beard. Shaan would always keep the protocol and refer to him as Prince in conversation to others, and call him "Sir" in direct conversation. By an act of providence and entirely unplanned as these things never are, Poncho and Shaan became good friends. As a result Shaan was invited aboard the Yacht Club with great frequency as a friend of the Founder – the Prince. Over the course of the next few days Shaan was also then invited to be a flat-mate of the Prince. He had a sprawling three bedroom penthouse with views of the Thames and Tower Bridge. The Prince was living by himself and was welcoming of some company. Things were looking up a little.

Things had been seeming to fall apart for Shaan, without anywhere to live, except with the proposition of maybe being under a bridge. Then Shaan got the offer to flat share with the Prince with a view of one of the most famous bridges in the world. As far as life's events go it was nothing short of "heaven's hand" as Shaan would come to refer to it. It would seem that "heaven's hand" was going to show itself more and more as and when the need would arise. The role of destiny, or Khama, in life is often an interesting one, as the Chinese say, "may you live in interesting times."

As Shaan accepted the offer, he also took the opportunity to make disclosure of who he was and also that there were criminal charges looming over him in the state of Florida, USA. The Prince took this in good heart and sitting with Shaan he shared his own family history, which was also quite racy. He was on his father's side the hereditary Prince from the principality of Sachin – which had been dissolved when the British left India. From his mother's side he was the oldest grandnephew of Zulfikar Ali Bhutto, the democratically elected Prime Minster who had been removed in a military coup d'ètat and then executed. His first cousin was the recently assassinated Prime Minister of Pakistan, Benazir Bhutto. The Princes three boys had actually been raised by Benazir when their mother had passed away when they were young. The family ties had been very close. You really could not find a person that could better understood how politics works and how ugly it can get. His offer to Shaan of support grew in leaps and bounds. He was one of those angels on earth that had stepped into Shaan's life and he remained steadfast throughout with dedicated resolve.

The Prince's club facilities were offered for Shaan's use, under the Prince's account, without any limitations for use in business or entertainment. These liberties were however used with guarded discretion. Kindness, as Shaan was taught early on in life was not to be abused, taken for granted or seen as weakness. The use of the private club facilities provided immense credibility to Shaan in his business dealings. Wani also was involved with Shaan in trying to develop commerce and contacts. Wani invited Shaan to a RuStyle cocktail monthly event. RuStyle was originally designed as a monthly social for Russian expats to meet for business, culture and entertainment. It had essentially become an event hosting expats – regardless of country of origin, but the name RuStyle stuck. The founders of RuStyle were two sisters from Latvia, the older was Nadia Bilinova. Nadia helpfully placed Shaan on the guest list without membership dues to every RuStyle event. This type of gathering/networking event lead several acquaintanceships and friendships. Two such friendships that grew from RuStlye were Anna Boyarova, also Latvian and Tom Day, whose family was in the hospitality business. They owned and operated boutique hotels in England, and their flagship hotel was in Derbyshire – the Izak Walton Hotel. Shaan would visit the Hotel for business meetings in northern England as required as a guest of the Day family.

Shaan and Tom had become friends and business colleagues.

As things continued to develop and mature it seemed more and more that the physical commodities trade business was full of nonsense. Everyone seemed to be working some scam or other, and never had the caveat emptor slogan been more appropriate. Shaan coined the phrase "there was so much bullshit in the international commodity trade,that if we could only lift and load the BS there would be a fortune to be made." As a matter of course Shaan's activities shifted into the natural adaptation of the business enterprises that were within his economic orbit - it was hospitality in general.

On a private occasion with Nicholas, one of the Prince's sons with whom Shaan had also grown particularly close, Shaan commented – "some people need titles to give them value – in your father's case he gives value to his title". In many respects the two men shared mutual admiration.

The Prince had noted Shaan's ability to engage and work with people. He often said he knew of no better personality to get people together, or a person that could get into any scene and be able to manage it better than Shaan. This was especially noted after Shaan had impromptu set up a meeting between himself at the famed Bollywood actor Shahrukh Khan during one of his shoots in London. Many more such unique dignitaries as a result of Shaan's "talent" as the Prince called it came on board the club, including Ken Warfe, Lady Diana's personal bodyguard and Oliver Rothschild to mention a few. As a result Shaan also began to represent the Yacht London Club at certain events and receptions such as at diplomatic cocktails including at the Russian Ambassador's residence for his farewell ball – an occasion where he met Mohamed Al-Fayed, at the time the owner of HARRODS and father of Doddi Al-Fayed, who had perished along with Princess Diana in that horrific accident in Paris some years earlier.

After some weeks the Prince made an offer to Shaan for a venture involving the Yacht London Club. The Yacht London Club was having non-functional weekends not producing any income. Noting this, the Prince offered to Shaan the rental of the facility to undertake whatever promotions Shaan wanted to, as long as the cost of operations for the facility were met. Shaan naturally took up the opportunity. It was real, tangible and here – better than any vague possibilities currently on the radar screen of business. First of all Shaan needed a name for this new entertainment enterprise. The facility was a yacht – it should at the least carry the name of a lady and a special lady – so he called it "Club ZOYA at the Yacht London". He named the venue and the enterprise after his daughter – there was no other lady more special to him.

A few new friends who knew all about Shaan and his history, like Darko Martin the General Manger of the Red Room, the private club of the Inter-Continental Hotel at the time helped Shaan to promote his weekend venue. Cassandra Tomaz – model / actress and the Miss Clairol Girl for the UK two years running had also befriended Shaan. Her beauty transcended the physical – she was charismatic with a magnetic kind caring personality. She most graciously and willingly provided her personage as the co-hostess at Shaan's side for the inaugural and all successive evenings. Cassandra was tremendous in arranging some of the entertainment too, DJ included. The idea was to create different themes for each Saturday night and varied themes for "Lazy Sunday's" The theme for the kick-off event was Arabian Nights – hookahs, belly dancers and food to match the genre. Tom Day also participated in the event getting his staff familiar with promotions to help out. Before the inaugural evening's events kicked off, Shaan managed to get the lady after whom he had named this club activity on a skype call – his daughter, Zoya. He spoke to his princess whom he also called his most precious, then to his son Zayn and finally to Amina. Then it was time to get back to task.

Tom had committed one person from his staff to assist Shaan through the logistics involved in setting up the event, and it was Yana Leonova. Tom was also the founder of a company that provided Human Resources to the hospitality industry branded under the domain name of www.hotelstaff.com. To meet the requirements of his jobseekers and placement needs he needed a Russian speaking staffer. He had been to Moscow to conduct interviews and in the process had identified a likely candidate for the position his company needed – Yana Leonova. Some weeks earlier Tom had been scheduled to pick Yana up from the airport at Heathrow on her arrival from Moscow and since he was at dinner with Shaan – he asked if Shaan would go along with him for sake of company. In a matter of weeks from arrival Yana provided significant operational support to Tom and Shaan. As unpredictable as life's business can be sometimes Yana and Shaan developed a friendship that would show its sincerity and commitment over time and distance.

All in all the first night boasted over 400 attendees – it was a success in that the program actually did not lose financially and actually made a slight profit. Things were moving in the right direction once again. Life was teaching that innovation, the ability to adapt and also a blessing from heaven could make all things possible, even ventures that had not ever been in contemplation.

Unfortunately time was beginning to run out in terms of Shaan's continued stay in the UK. He had arrived nearly six months before and he had no desire to remain in violation of the UK Border laws. He spoke with solicitors recommended by Cassandra but it had become too late to process any immigration petitions. The only possibility was to leave the UK and then step back in again. This would normally be a fairly straightforward process.

So Shaan went ahead on a Monday morning, after the weekend of a ZOYA event on the Yacht London had concluded, and went off to Kings Cross Train Station and bought a ticket to Paris, France. He was going to do his popping out and stepping back in routine. It was literally the day before his 180 days was going to be up. Another trip, another destination, another possibility.

Shahrukh Khan (Bollywood Superstar) and Shahrukh Dhanji
At the wrap up party after a shoot in London

Shahrukh Dhanji with Ken Warfe (Princess Diana's Head of Security)

Chapter 12. *Journey to Lithuania.*

Travel brings power and love back into your life."
— Rumi

If this was always true then Shaan should have been on top of the world, rather than as the Hungarian's say "under the frog's arse". Shaan arrived in Paris, the city of romance as they say, – and he had stepped out of the UK just before the expiration of the 180 days' time limit and in doing so was abiding by the UK Border guidelines, at no time did he wish to transgress the laws of his host countries. His simple plan was to return the same day later in the evening. Shaan was unfortunately not actually aware that it was not just a step out and step back in procedure. It is different for a visitor from the USA and UK Border guidelines required that you can only stay 6 months out of every 12 months in the UK, unlike many Europeans who can come and go. It was a risky maneuver for Shaan to say the least – but the risks were simply not known. If by some chance Shaan did get back through then a new 180 days cycle (6 month period) would start again and then there would be time to file the necessary immigration petitions, and keep the business operations on the Yacht London going on the weekends. Sometimes things don't work out as you hope.

And so Shaan spent the day wandering around Paris, taking in the sights, and reported back in time for the boarding of the night train back to London. Unfortunately the UK Border and Customs was at the train station, Paris- Nord. He got in line filled out the appropriate entry forms for UK Border and presented himself to the next UK Border Officer. The slightly bored looking official scrutinized the American passport with care, and then denied Shaan re-entry into the UK, based on the 6 month out of 12 month rule which was news to Shaan. It was to say the least a moment of deafening silence – at least for Shaan while the rest of the station was still in its full glory of the hustle and bustle. So here he was – there were no options of a return to the London, and no one knew he had left the country as Shaan had expected to be back within 24 hours. Now he was in seriously unchartered territory, he had no contacts or local knowledge– he had not been in a spot so precarious before and had no desire to be found in it again.

Still Paris is also sometimes called the city of dreams, so maybe something might turn up?

If troubles make you stronger then Shaan was by now the Iron Knight, but now it was becoming a fight for personal survival rather than anything else. It was raining cats and dogs that night in Paris as he stepped back out of the Train station to find a hotel room. It was late, and he only had some British Pounds on him – he hadn't taken the trouble to change money as he had not expected to be marooned in Paris. He walked the empty streets in the rain till he found one of the many small hotels that had a lamp on inside. He rang the bell and someone opened the door and in he stepped from the rainy wet cold of Paris. The man on the front desk was a middle-aged man and he spoke rather remarkably good English. After some initial questions and pleasantries the man asked Shaan if he was American, as he said noticing his accent, something that isn't always a good sign in France. Shaan replied he was indeed and after some more chat the hotelier then announced that he had spent 10 years living in Boca Raton, Florida – and strangely the world suddenly got a whole lot smaller and looked better. Kharma moves in mysterious ways and off all the people in Paris to run into at a time like this – he had accidentally found a fellow Floridian. Shaan confirmed that he too was indeed a Floridian and further explained his immediate, rather odd, predicament. Hoteliers have heard most things but this got him a room with the leave to get the British Pounds converted to Euro's the following day. This was a small hotel and they did not provide currency exchange, but they had a bit of the old fashioned personal touch. The room was certainly more pleasant than the ghastly one he had in London when he first arrived there from Bangkok. It seemed that Heaven's Hand had intervened once more. Whatever this journey had evolved into, it was personally clear to Shaan it was not by his design. He was in a journey philosophically speaking that was in the flow of the river and it felt like he had no control of the rivers current.

The next day Shaan went to the British Embassy which unfortunately confirmed the border control laws, and the fact that he wouldn't be allowed back in for six months. The next step then was the US Embassy, he needed to figure out what his local options might be in legal terms, or where he could go. In Paris, like in so many places in the world, some of the external gated security of American Embassies is managed by local private security companies – at least until you get through the outer protection perimeter – then off-course the Marines and the RSO (regional Security Officer) functionaries takeover. Shaan was immediately told by the private security staff that he needed an appointment to get into the Embassy to meet with anyone. In typical form Shaan then forcibly informed the security personnel that he was an American, that the security staffer was not – and he certainly was not going to take directives from a non-American to get to see a DOS (Department of State) staffer at the American Embassy. That fairly belligerent approach resulted in Shaan being ushered through to a communications booth where the Consular in Charge of Citizen Services came on the line. He took Shaan's passport number over the phone and confirmed that there was unfortunately no other means of managing the situation with the British regulations, and told him that this seemed to occur more frequently than one might have expected. It seemed that 3 to 5 American were turned back every week for overstaying in the British Isles, and Shaan had simply become one of them.

What was really interesting was that the Consular officer did nothing to invite Shaan onto Embassy grounds or to alert the RSO (Regional Security Officer) – after all there was a warrant for his arrest in Florida and that should have been placed on the NCIC grid. This alert, which means that he was wanted man, and his passport identification should have tripped the alert but it did not – or if it did the Consular did not care to get involved, despite his requirement to do so.

That evening of his first full day in Paris, which had not exactly been romantic, Shaan reached out to his good friend, back in London, the Prince. He was quite concerned as he did not know where Shaan had been, they were after all close friends and flat-mates. Shaan basically explained what had happened and that he had not expected to be out of London for more than 24 hours. Shaan was, of course, short of funds and made no mention to the Prince of this, but the Prince without discussing it offered Shaan an immediate contact in Paris, who handed over to Shaan a few hundred Euros at the Prince's request.

That friendship and generosity bought Shaan a few more days to figure out what to do. Other friends like Cassandra, Wani, Anna Boyarova and Mobin Fadshafar all expressed concern and offered various forms of support and resources from Solicitor's to assist in his return to wired funds if needed. The offers were most appreciated and showed the sincerity of friendship that had evolved. The time in Paris was short – less than a week. Time was essentially spent trying to assess the next most viable prudent action – and it had to happen fast. Ultimately it was Tom Day who came up with a useful, immediate and viable solution. After a couple of days Tom confirmed through his solicitors that the best thing to do was stay out of Britain for the required six months and then on return to the UK file the papers necessary for an business or employment type visa. In the meantime Tom also offered Shaan the chance to go to Spain. Tom's family had a five bedroom villa in Moraira, between Valencia and Alicante which had a view of the Mediterranean. He told Shaan he could go down there and stay in the Villa for as long as was necessary. In terms of exile this wasn't so bad and at least this way there would be a place to stay and he could start to sort things out from there. Shaan took up the offer and headed off by train from Paris to Valencia. What should have been a half day train journey turned into an all day journey. The French had one of their usual strikes and the trains stopped working for about four hours. The train Shaan was on came to a stop in Montpellier in France, close to the Mediterranean coast and near to Spain. When the trains finally started running again Shaan found himself in Barcelona, late at night and within 30 minutes of the Train station closing and, of course, the connecting train to Valencia would not be running till early the next morning. Out of options and unable to stay in the train terminal since it was closing, Shaan purchased a ticket for a local train to head into the city center and spend the night some where, not knowing where. Funds were indeed rather scant. As he walked towards the local train terminal there he saw two South Asian looking young men – and as it goes in new lands immigrant eyes met with as a sign of noted recognition – it seems the same the world over. Then, as it turned out these men were from Pakistan and here too heaven's hand reached out again. Not only was there the visual recognition but a passing word of greeting, "salam" (which means "Peace") – that alone was enough to start a short conversation before the local train arrived. Eventually the two men invited Shaan back to their flat for the night for food and rest and the evening turned from desolation to one of companionship and respite. In a moment of reflection it seemed that just as Shaan had stood to support and protect various cultures, races and groups as a Commissioner in Florida – life was showing they too could come to his support from corners previously unknown, but by the grace of heaven's hand, or of Kharma. The next morning one of them woke Shaan and accompanied him through the maze of the train metro in Barcelona to make sure Shaan got on the scheduled train to Valencia.

From Valencia to Moraira he went by taxi to the property manager's office held the keys for Tom's family villa. They were expecting him and had been instructed to convey the keys and access to Shaan on his arrival. So this was Shaan's fourth or fifth country of exile and meant once more trying to acclimatize to the local culture and find ways of doing business. This was like a Global MBA with bells on it.

But the quest, the old challenge to make it back home to Florida, with the intention to have the funds necessary for a return and a fight seemed to be slipping away. It had been nearly 2 years, 3 continents and 6 countries since Shaan's flight had begun. Relationships were made along the way and thankfully retained. It was indeed beginning to feel like an Odyssey, with America as the one-eyed Cyclops. Shaan was searching for the Golden Fleece but it was proving difficult to locate. Business operations seemed to get ready to up and go and the next thing that happened in time is that it was time to get up and go. So the only thing that actually was in "go" mode, was Shaan, somebody kept moving the starting line, the finishing line and even the race-track.

Moraira is a small holiday town directly on the Mediterranean on the Costa Blanca (White Coast) region of Spain, half way between Alicante and Valencia. It was a typical Spanish port-town, small white houses and old-cobbled streets running down to the sea. The whole town was literally three small streets lined with café's, boutiques and now banks as well all leading directly to the waterfront of the Mediterranean Sea. A yacht club that was surrounded by overhanging cliffs cut away from mountains and small alleys with traditional style restaurants. It was a picture from a Mediterranean coast town lost in time from the 19th century, but busily partaking in the new global wealth that energizes places like this. Shaan took his usual daily walk down from the Villa with his small laptop with bag slung over his shoulder. There was no wifi connection in the Villa so it was necessary to walk down to a local café, a not unpleasant way of linking to the outside world. The point was to keep in contact with friends and contacts and to try and keep business possibilities alive. So maintaining lines of communication were essential. His first attempt of communication was with Amina and the kids, to know they were fine and safe was always paramount.

That first Sunday of Shaan's stay he decided to find out what Moraira was all about – what could it offer. During his walk he found only one store front open on a late warm sunny Sunday afternoon. It was a new real estate office opened by the owner of Alitrend Realty, Diego Periea, who, it turned out, had another office on the other side of town. He wanted one on each end for the obvious reason to have a better reach for new customers. So, despite being Sunday, Shaan went in to find that the office was staffed by a lady behind the reception desk. Shaan stepped in to say hello – there wasn't much else happening in this sleepy town on a Sunday afternoon. He was expecting to hear Spanish - instead he heard a reply to his "hello" in clear American English. He had stumbled upon probably the only other American in town. The two talked for a couple of hours and the coffee kept pouring into the cups – courtesy of Diego's office and the efforts of Shaan's fellow American, Lynda Ceen. Shaan met Diego and his new wife Sonia later that evening when they came to check the new office and help close it for the evening. To Shaan they looked the ideal couple out of a classic Hollywood movie, perfectly attired and in perfect step with each other. Diego's good looks were matched by his character, noble and genuinely sincere as time would come to prove.

It had been nearly two weeks since Shaan had left London on his day-trip. Not planning on being out for more than a day all he had was the set of clothing on his back he had left London with. That required a hand wash every evening – air dry and re-ironed shirt and trouser in the morning, and a jacket every day. It seemed his childhood upbringing and navy training of staying presentable and inspection ready at all times had stayed with him. Shaan had by open invitation visited daily the only other American, Lynda and she was just as pleased to speak to him in English, (American-style off-course) a language it seemed only the two of them shared in this town and as it became clear in time the surrounding towns too. Diego would visit, and through the natural evolution in friendly conversations everyone got to know each more and more. Lynda did her own Google research on Shaan and one-day flat out asked him he was the fellow that was wanted in Florida. Shaan's response was to directly reply yes, since this was obviously the only sensible thing to do. From that point on Lynda familiarized herself with his case and the facts surrounding it, including the Futch email. Their friendship only got stronger as a result of this honesty and sharing of information.

Diego needed someone else in his office with Lynda and asked Shaan if he would help out. In less than a month Shaan was once again making enough money to survive and sent back all that he could for his kids. It was still a difficult time however. Tom's sister was coming down with her family for a vacation in Spain and Shaan had to find alternative accommodation. Very simply Diego offered up one of his villas - it was larger and within a hop and skip of the Mediterranean coastline. The property was laden with orange trees. So at time when it was not possible to buy water from the market "heaven's hand" reached down and made available fresh orange juice. Like any traveler Shaan took the rough with the smooth and enjoyed this.

Shaan was still seeking to re-establish a substantial income stream out of reach of the Satz-Miller tentacles as were deployed under color of law, and lest we forget FDLE Agent James Futch. Back in Florida the powerful political few were in their comfort zone now – the Challenger had at least as it seemed been flung out permanently and presented no danger to them.

Three months passed with daily reporting to Diego's office. Various friends from London frequently visited to check in on Shaan. They included Cassandra Tomaz, Anna Boyarova, Yana Leonova, Tom Day and Samuel Dehaney. Samuel was a real estate agent in London and so he and Shaan explored creating a real estate connection between the UK and Spain for buyers and sellers. Samuel also had a side hobby which he made some money from – he was a dead ringer for the movie actor Samuel L. Jackson. This got him gigs and lots of fun at the lounges, a kind of appearance money in our celebrity obsessed culture. From the many friends that visited and kept in touch it was abundantly apparent that a family was being created in the journey of life. Lynda took on a voluntary effort to expose the corrupt investigation and its results by posting material on the Internet. It was a gesture most noble but ultimately it did not succeed, the power of truth is often over-rated. Despite some impact not much spurred from it to really help Shaan. By December, it was Shaan's birthday, and he got the amazing gift of real hot dogs, home baked cupcakes and a Happy Birthday rendition from Lynda and her two daughters. It was an oddly poignant moment and a sincere and heartfelt occasion. That Christmas of 2011 left an indelible mark on Shaan, particularly since it was such a difficult time to be separated from his family, another year. Time had only made the pain of separation more piercing. That Christmas, Diego for the first time in his life invited someone from outside his family to Christmas dinner, he invited Shaan. At that dinner he called Shaan "Hermano" (Brother) and coming from Diego it was a real honor and privilege, it was not something done so easily to have Diego bring someone into his family. The friendship and respect matured into a familial affection, and so it remains.

While in Moraira many developments occurred. Bob Norman, the South Florida newspaper writer wrote an article about Shaan in a local South Florida newspaper, referring to Shaan as the "International Man of Mystery", International he had been and had become even more so, but there was nothing mysterious about him. In fact Shaan was still as tenacious as ever in wanting to regain strength and get back home to the fight he so believed in.

Around this time Shamsuddin, the emotionally disturbed and narcotic dependent son of Amina from her first marriage e-mailed Shaan asking for forgiveness and understanding, and saying that he had cleaned himself up. This was the recurring modus operandi of Shamsuddin – stay straight, fall of the track – let time pass, make the apologies and try again, or atleast make a show pretending to. Shaan although recognizing this pattern always felt affection for this lad and wrote back that he was glad for him. It seemed Shamsuddin had fallen in love with a German girl who was visiting India and the two had decided to get married and he wanted to come to Europe. He asked Shaan to help him with a visa and the request was successfully obliged. Ultimately, the possibility of matrimony faded after he visited the girl and her family in Germany. He then returned to Spain to be with Shaan and it seemed his adopted habits of drug dependency had not in fact left him, and this dependency brought on other issues of behavioral instability as well. Shamsuddin recognized the inner conflicts that were driving him and decided to move out on his own. Here again history repeated for the third time just as easily as their life journey's had crossed so again it uncrossed.

Shaan had helped get Shamsuddin into Europe for many reasons, certainly there was the desire to help the lad get on with life. It was also to try and set the stage so he could see his children. He thought that Amina would certainly want to meet her son whom she had not seen for four years now. If she would come to

Spain to meet her son, Shaan thought he would also be able to meet his children that he so pined for without interruption. In fact, Diego and George Saliba had secured airline tickets and reservations for Amina and the kids to fly over to Spain for a visit. As usual however Amina, decided that she would not come.

By now in fact Amina had also filed for divorce and the courts had granted it. Communication responses were infrequent, despite Shaan's daily messages on email and Skype. In failing of female company for over two years, Shaan indulged in an intimate relationship. He needed to feel like all men do and a Moroccan lady had taken a liking to him. It lasted all but a short two months– it was not an emotional entanglement that either Shaan of the lady were looking for.

Time after time he had openly shared with Amina that he had wanted only her in his life but that it seemed every time any effort was made in the past two and half years she only found a reason not to keep the matrimonial bond alive. No doubt she had faced much in the past two and half years, but she took it on herself to do this alone. For reasons not clear she discarded relationships and friendships that she and Shaan had built together. She dispensed with regular contact with Shaan's parents and with close friends like John and Janet Sims, Howard and Donna Gressmen and others. She simply withdrew into a zone of people confined by her religious and cultural familiarity. Still she had been through much more than anyone could have foreseen, and she had done the best possible as we each do by our own understanding and strengths. She would remain always in affection, by Shaan – after all it was her womb that brought the most valued lives in Shaan's world into being. Despite vows of commitment and loyalty at weddings, adversity and trauma however is not what people expect in marriage and so Amina had withdrawn.

George Saliba, the untiring good friend from Florida had business ventures developing though a Private Banking relationship in Madrid and so he regularly visited Spain. From his first trip to Spain and every successive trip he always reached out to Shaan and the two always met, whether in Moraira or Madrid. George had been the one friend who had not only kept in touch but actually made visits to meet Shaan in these past two years. In a short time Shaan was introduced to Miguel Artilles, the Chief Executive at Bandenia, a Private Bank. The bank wanted to set-up an E-Banking platform and had heard that Lithuania would be conducive for this type of activity. It transpired that Barclays from the UK had just set-up some of their e-banking facilities in Lithuania as well. George having a close relationship to Miguel and Bandenia suggested they retain Shaan as the consultant to go to Lithuania and start the initial assessment. This was agreed and Shaan was retained and the project got underway.

There was just one major issue – Shaan had no valid passport for travel, in fact his passport had expired. He had sent it off to the American Embassy in Madrid for renewal but all he got back was notification that he would need to come into the US Embassy for a personal interview to get his passport. This was a glaring red flag as large as could be waived for Shaan. It was saying come on over so we can have the RSO take you into custody, and off you can go back to Florida. Going to Florida was not the issue, being able to prevail in a legal battle to take those into account for violating their public trust was. The time was still not right and Shaan was not prepared to walk into the lion's den unarmed.

After consultation it was decided to try and bypass this problem by driving to Lithuania, and hopefully getting through the borders without a passport. So a vehicle with a driver was arranged to take Shaan to Lithuania. The journey was not going to be without incident or the intervention of "Heaven's Hand". Like Ulysses before him Shaan set off on yet another difficult journey designed to finally bring home to his own hearth, but there were more complications.

Shaan had kept his Hermano, Diego apprised of his aims and intentions and Diego had wished Shaan well in this endeavor, and told him that there would always be a home for him in Moraira. Every journey starts with one small step but soon becomes a laborious and lengthy process. It was February of 2012 and not a good time to be driving across Europe. The winter was harsh and road travel had to go fairly slowly and steadily. From southern Spain to Lithuania is a very long, and difficult drive. The designated driver and car with Shaan ensconced in it left Madrid on this arduous road trek to Lithuania. It would take them through the whole of Spain, France, Germany, Poland and then to the country of destination. The travel was planned without stopping except for the fuel fill-up. The driver, whilst being an amiable chap, was not accustomed to the icy roads and he had managed to skid and hit a side railing off the road. That resulted in dents to the front driver's side fender and it knocked out the front left headlight, but it was not damage enough to stop and get repairs, according to the driver, and so the drive continued. Neither Shaan nor the driver knew that the Germans only like vehicles on their roads that are in top condition and undamaged. As the frontier into Germany was crossed the German border police noting the damage to the vehicle came alongside and had the car pulled over for a stop and check. The stop and check included checking the occupants of the car, the driver had his identification, but all Shaan had was a copy of the picture page of an expired American passport. Murphy's Law was in full force and effect, and with people not noted for their sense of humour.

The German police then took the car and both the driver and Shaan into custody and brought them back to their station. The driver was released without much delay – his identity papers were clear and had checked out. Shaan on the other hand was a different story. It was of course a Saturday and the Germans said they needed to check his identity with the US Embassy on Monday and that they would as a result have to hold Shaan over the weekend. Shaan was then taken into a cell – fully equipped with a cement slab for a bed. It has to be said that the German Police were absolute gentlemen in their communication to and treatment of Shaan. He asked for water, a couple of sheets to lay down on the slab and one to put over him like a blanket. They were fine about all this and obliged.

As he lay there in his cell he thought back over the past 3 years. It seemed ironic to think that this struggle and fight was going to end because of a traffic stop owing to a broken headlight and dented fender. It made no sense and Shaan's prayer was a question to the Creator of all that is in the Heavens and on Earth. If all this was going to end here like this in Germany then he told God, it had all been a bad joke and God – you will be the only one laughing. Shaan's prayer was – if I am on the right path and if my intentions clear and correct then let me finish this journey in good conscience.

Somehow or other in less than 45 minutes the German police came and opened the door to Shaan's cell. Now believe what you will about German efficiency but they said to Shaan we have checked with our Chief, we have researched the computer systems and we find no reason to hold you. We are going to release you and provide you with a temporary German State identity card in case if you are stopped for any reason. The Identity card was valid for two weeks, and they actually said to Shaan, enjoy Germany for the two weeks but please make sure that you leave before the two weeks are up.

The police did not fingerprint Shaan and nor did they take a photograph for their systems. The picture they used on the identity card was provided by Shaan. He had kept passport size pictures with him in his computer bag, extra pictures he had taken for the renewal of his US Passport, if that ever happened.

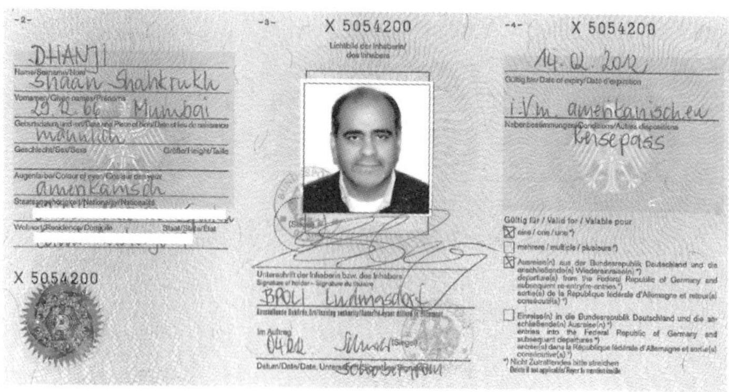
-2-

DHANJI

Shaan Shahrukh

29. 12. 66 Mumbai

männlich

amerikanisch

X 5054200

-3- X 5054200

Unterschrift der Inhaberin bzw. des Inhabers

Signature of holder – Signature du titulaire

Im Auftrag

-4- X 5054200

14. 02. 2012

i.V.m. amerikanischem Reisepass

Gültig für / Valid for / Valable pour

[X] eine / one / une *)

[ ] mehrere / multiple / plusieurs *)

[X] Ausreise(n) aus der Bundesrepublik Deutschland und die anschließende(n) Wiedereinreise(n) *)
departure(s) from the Federal Republic of Germany and subsequent re-entry(re-entries) *)
sortie(s) de la République fédérale d'Allemagne et retour(s) consécutif(s) *)

[ ] Einreise(n) in die Bundesrepublik Deutschland und die anschließende(n) Ausreise(n) *)
entries into the Federal Republic of Germany and subsequent departures *)
entrée(s) dans la République fédérale d'Allemagne et sortie(s) consécutive(s) *)

*) Nicht Zutreffendes bitte streichen

German issued Pass / Travel Document. Almost three Years to the Date since Shaan had left to go to Hungry

The Driver and Shaan walked over to the car – started it and continued on with the journey, as though nothing had happened. It was travel time that gave Shaan much space to reflect on the process of moving forward. He had in conscience and law done nothing wrong, but was now a constant fugitive. He had taken on a fight for something he believed in – the Constitution of the United States and the preservation of democratic values from the blemish of the politically corrupt few. He had made the decision much earlier on in challenging what had happened – now he felt something had to give. It was still unclear as to how that challenge would be conducted – except that it had too. It was absolutely ludicrous that he was targeted, maligned and that but for the failure of funds Shaan could not fight back. To wear injustice and have no means to challenge the wrong that had been done was demoralizing, yet bred resistance.

But what Shaan was fighting for was right and within the law. What he wanted was a safe harbor from which to fight back, and so the law in its independent and broad power alone would have to provide the answer fuelled by personal will, tenacity and conviction. This ultimate stand to bring this matter of corruption to light would make its fight and exposure under the provisions of European Union law as administered by an ally of the United States, the Republic of Lithuania.

Chapter 13. *Safe Harbour and the Sharpening of Justice's Broad Sword.*

The arrival in Lithuania was late in the evening, and by the time the driver and Shaan rolled into Vilnius it was already past midnight. The checked in to the Europa City Hotel, next to which was the American fast food icon KFC. It was a cold night, both driver and Shaan were exhausted – all they wanted and needed was a bed to land on. They next morning they woke to the typical winter weather of the Baltics. Snow flurries and gray skies. Shaan had, after being retained by Bandenia, already undertaken some research to make contacts with the central Banking Authority in Lithuania. He wanted to get direct access and the information of registration requirements for the e-banking platform for his client. He also through a distinguished social media platform called asmallworld (by membership only) of which Shaan was a member made contact with a commercial lawyer in Vilnius, for legal support.

Shaans, German experience had stayed very much alive with him and it was time to act. If not directly back in the USA, then through a recognized and honored friend of the US. A place where the law was viewed and respected, indeed a venue that was an ally of the US. Afterall Shaan's fight had been for the preservation of American ideals and not for tearing them down. Although not apparent at the time, Shaan, born in the largest Democracy in the World (India), who had sworn to protect and defend the strongest Democracy in the world (USA) was now going to seek protection from the first Democracy to break away from the Soviet Union (Lithuania).

Sometimes the omens felt better than at other times.

Shaan asked his lawyer to contact the authorities and to pose a hypothetical – would Lithuania consider extending protection to an American if it was deemed the law in the United States as applied was a violation of Human Rights laws, of due process, was political and selective in application. The lawyer laughed and was not taking Shaan seriously, and suggested that Lithuania would never take such an action if it would be deemed to take a stand that might even appear to be politically against America. After the years of communism and oppression the idea of standing up to the most powerful country in the world to protect a new visitor did seem like a very foolish notion.

But for Shaan the lawyer had missed the point. To be American meant doing the right thing, it meant upholding human rights and it meant the preservation of the law. It was not draping oneself in the color of a flag only to forget what it stood for – and the lives sacrificed over the years for the values and principles of ideology represented by the flag. Post-communist cynicism didn't really extend to the ideas of truth and liberty, merely to survival and opportunity.

In a few short days while still managing Bandenia's affairs, that included ascertaining banking licensing requirements, consideration of acquisition of assets and possible retention of employees of a failed bank in the region were part of the professional and retained activities. Shaan had met some individuals, one of them was a recently graduated law graduate named Jan, who was acting as Shaan's translator. With Jan, Shaan went to the Vilnius District Migration Office where also was located the office of the Chief of Migration Police. Shaan presented himself, asked for Protection, and made it amply clear he was not here to surrender - but to present himself for protection.

A statement was then taken from Shaan, it lasted nearly 3 hours. He was electronically fingerprinted and photographed. When it was all over, he asked if he was going to be held or he could return to his abode. The senior in charge looked at him and declared- you had enough honor to come here, I think if I call you will have enough honor to return. Shaan smiled, thanked him and went back to his place of residence, the slightly grimy flat in down-town. He had moved out of the hotel to take on a temporary apartment that was far more economical – it was going to take some weeks to get the Bandenia's requirement assessed and confirmed. In about 8 weeks the Bandenia report was completed and submitted. Unfortunately because of the lack of appropriate travel documents Shaan remained behind in Lithuania.

For god or bad – the system of law was now in effect. Lithuania would administer the law, but the law was predicated by the European Union. Lithuania had 72 hours to make a decision to provide a review of the assertions made by Shaan, or simply have him removed back to the USA, since the US was categorized as a "Safe Country". On the very last day the Migration Police contacted Shaan and asked him to come in – they said they had some more questions to ask him. To Shaan this was the call to come in and be taken into custody. At this juncture he was ready – he was in the hands of God, just as he had recently been in Germany and in so many personally challenging situations before. He took his translator Jan and they headed off to the Migration Police Department. They took the elevator up to the third floor entered the appropriate office and announced their arrival. A migration official asked Shaan to join him at her desk. There were no questions, simply they asked Shaan to sign on of the documentary forms that was inadvertently left out when he had come to make his declaration a couple of days earlier. They said they would let him know their decision in some days – no final decision had been made. It was 4 pm in the afternoon. Shaan and his translator left the third floor and went down to call a taxi. Before the taxi arrived, Shaan's cell phone rang, it was the Migration officer he had just left. They asked him to return. Shaan had been approved for the first 90 days of protection while his case was to be reviewed. It was a first for an American. Shaan went straight up to the office he had left. More papers were prepared and signed and stamped and he was asked to go the following day to the office where Asylum and Refugee cases were adjudicated. He did so and that next day Shaan received his first 90 day Foreigner Registration Document – it was serialized USA -0001.

First ID Card issued by Lithuania while Investigating Shaan and the investigation that charged him

Typically, only two 90 day periods are provided – within which time a decision would have to be made. In Shaan's matter the periods would extend to five and some days. Shaan made initial submissions to the Migration office in charge of Asylum - it became very apparent in the second 90 day period (Periods 1 and 2) that the officer and supervisor in charge of the investigation were simply not going to make any decision that in the simple minded terms was politically anti-American. This was a typical position by the general public which likes to blindly drape itself in the color of the flag – not remembering what the colors are there to represent and uphold. For Shaan as it should be for any rational and prudent thinking person, it is anti-American to disregard the law and that the law is the constant - not the people representing it whether by sincerity or disingenuously. There is nothing honorable or noble in the American ideal by waving the flag but desecrating everything it stands for.

While the process was ongoing in Lithuania, Shaan was also working with Mark Hirsch, a lawyer introduced to him by his friend George Saliba. Shaan wanted to see if the FBI would take on the case, after all the Futch email was self-admitting to political will sabotaging the criminal justice system. But the FBI agent in charge of Public Corruption wanted more evidence. He wanted Shaan to out the case together for him. In any event the FBI Agent needed time to go and get back from the Republican Presidential National Convention, to which he was a delegate. The law had been put on hold and corruption in Florida could continue unchecked because the FBI agent in charge of public corruption had to get the National Republican Convention. He said this directly to Shaan over a Skype call that had been arranged by Mark Hirsch in his office. The fundamentals of democracy includes the essential right of participation in the election process. It is after all also what Shaan's fight was about too.

But here there certainly was not going to be any surprise that Mitt Romney was going to be the Republican nominee for President.

It was an oddly dire set of circumstances. The law was on holiday, of all places at a political party's national convention. This could have been written by Mark Twain, a great writer who loved the idiosyncrasies of the American way of doing things!

Through US lawyers, first Mark Hirsch, Shaan found out the Bond set for him was in excess of 200,000 USD. Similar charges would normally barely place a bond of 10,000 USD. The position argued by Satz's deputy Donnelly was that Shaan was a flight risk. Flight Risk? What risk – Shaan was already in flight. If he was to return of his own volition where would be the risk of flight? Rosenbaum who had kept in touch with Shaan over the years was surprised to learn that the Bond had been set so high, he was still Shaan's attorney of record and any bond hearing on this matter should have included him – and he had not been notified.

Rosenbaum sent over his investigator to the courthouse to "pull" the file on Shaan – no file could be found. What was going on here? Just exactly what FDLE Agent Futch's email had declared: "powerful political people wanted to see this man arrested". The bad guys had circled their wagons for protection – and actively doing what they needed to do to cover their tracks and obstruct disclosure. Missing files, and tapes, have a special place in American history.

Just as the second 90 day period was coming to a close, internal security investigation into the Migration Department in Lithuania resulted in arrests – it seemed that some of the officers were taking bribes for processing case files faster and favorably to the desires of the petitioner. In total about 13 people were arrested, suspended or removed from their positions. It caused for a complete re-shuffling of personnel. At least someone somewhere was taking corruption seriously and then doing something about it.

Shaan's file was re-assigned to a new investigator – Viktor Ostrovnoj. They had an initial meeting where Shaan asked Viktor a direct question. If you are going to make a political decision, we can go and pack my bags now and save everyone lots of time and resources, if you are going to make a legal decision then lets proceed – which is it going to be? Viktor, looked intensely with unwavering resolve in his eyes - He said the decision would be a legal one.

It would have taken a full five 90 day periods, as each period came closer to an end and for possible renewal or denial the anxiety levels elevated – it was an elongated period of uncertainty. What gave Shaan a sense of comfort were friends made almost from the beginning of his arrival in Lithuania, in particular whom he would refer to as the "Lithuanian Brothers" that frequented the Cigar Club in Vilnius's Old Town near daily, and the owner of the establishment is Kestutis Skerbys. Kestutis had been the former Minister of Interior at the time Lithuania had declared its independence in that turbulent period of the Soviet Union's demise. He and others Shaan met there would become his much needed personal support network - his "Lithuanian Brothers".

This time in Lithuania brought about finally a meeting with Shaan and his Father. It had been nearly 4 years since he had actually seen any member of his family. It was a brief visit of 3 weeks but it was what was most needed to give spirit and moral support. It had been a lone trail for the most part.

Shaan started to organize the evidentiary submissions, again. Over the course of the next two 90 day periods

(Periods 4 and 5) the evidence through an independent, internationally legally recognized system and process of law determined the Shahrukh Shiraz Dhanji – Shaan to his friends was indeed entitled to and was going to be afforded protection from open criminal charges on the state of Florida under the laws of the European Union, as administered by the Republic of Lithuania.

It was a simple analogy as Shaan had pointed out. Lithuania is the doctor that can treat a cancer called corruption, that cancer of corruption exist in the body of your friend the USA in a place called Florida. Won't you help your friend? The analogy worked because the facts supported it – the law looked at the evidence and administered for the protection of due process and human rights.

Although the corruption in the state of Florida is well documented and often recognized as unchecked – for the first time it reached the international stage. An American was granted a unique form of protection – Subsidiary Protection because something not correct had happened in the state of Florida.

The position and determination - To Stand and Fight – had prevailed in favor of the wronged. For Shaan it was vindication at a global level.

This vindication for Shaan also reciprocally served as a clear indictment against the parties involved in the investigation that targeted him. It was in the process of an independent third party critical review of the facts not allegations that rendered the decision to provide Shaan with protection, and thus condemning his opponents for the tainted and corrupt investigation.

Finally the wind changed and was at Shaan's back. If not through economics but by sheer will of doing what's right under the law was bringing on a change. Assuredly, the return to his home was beginning. Now the fight had to be brought home – to challenge and pursue those under the law that have acted only to make the law subservient to them. The ship of law and truth was headed to a port in Florida.

EPILOGUE

Shaan's "Protection" status continues to extend with additional periods under the law of the European Union as administered by the Republic of Lithuania. The continuity of protection that he enjoys on the international stage serves to openly expose the corruption that has indeed resulted from the transgression of law and an assassination of the democratic electoral process in Florida by "powerful political people". The damage to the values upon which a democratic society are principled is irreparable if in fact appropriate authority on notice of this matter fails to action. Officials on the state of Florida to include the Governor, Attorney General and Inspector General have all been notified by Shaan's attorney of this matter. To date the Governor has failed to acknowledge receipt of his letter, the Inspector General acknowledged receipt of the correspondence and the Attorney Generals response was that her office had no oversight on this alleged corruption – this coming from the chief executive in charge of protecting all the people in the state of Florida under the law - was to say the least, surprisingly shocking – she referred the matter to the Governor's office. It seems that State Attorneys that have remained in office as long as Satz extend an invisible hand of malign influence that touched even the capital of the state. The many acts of wrongdoing continue and the more notorious from time to time percolates through exposure, although many are inured to such things. Most recently scandals concerning the current Sheriff of Broward County – Scott Israel are surfacing. Israel's interest in a private security company –Talon/G6 was in partnership with a former Hollywood police chief neatly called Scarberry, (Hollywood PD - AGAIN) who gained notoriety in 2007 after federal prosecutors said they were forced prematurely to shut down a two-year FBI undercover investigation of police corruption in Hollywood after Scarberry leaked word of the probe. "We were betrayed by the police chief," retired FBI agent Jack Garcia told *Miami Herald* columnist Fred Grimm in 2008.

When Israel sold his shares in Talon / G6 the buyer was tied to the scandal that had removed Jenne as Sheriff of Broward County under corruption charges on a Federal indictment. The more things changed the more they stayed the same – the players just got moved around a little and the political apparatus of the powerful political few was not disrupted.

In the absence active of Federal intervention in this matter, Florida will continue to bloom in the wicked garden of corruption.

Shaan's legal rebirth has once again fueled his passion in the areas of Human Rights, Conflict Prevention and Education. He has established a private not for profit foundation in support of these interest under his family name – "Dhanji Foundation". (www.dhanjifoundation.com).

Shaan continues in his legal battle against the "powerful political people" – the corrupt, who officiated in their positions to transgress the very law they themselves were sworn to uphold and defend – for the preservation of democratic ideals and an electoral process that is fundamental to a society under the law.

His personal prayer remains unification with his children.

ACKNOWLEDGEMENTS

By: Shahrukh Dhanji – (Shaan)

I have been graced by the kindness of heaven to encounter and call friend certain people in this journey that has spanned five years. Many have been mentioned in the book, many still have not. Most will remain the silent hero's that passed through my life providing me the benefit of a smile or the simple indulgence of conversation. It kept me going. My grateful recognition and sincere Thank-You.

But there are some that warrant and merit mention or I would fail in conscience. Foremost I am compelled time and time again to note that the love for and from my children has been the empowerment of my resolve and resilience. They have laid a sacrifice in the early years of their life that was not of their calling. It is my prayer that the conclusion of at least this chapter of life will leave them a better society – and selfishly for me time with them endearingly again for countless more chapters in life, yet to be written.

By far an overwhelming abundance of gratitude to my parents. My father and mother have exemplified the standard of parenthood. Full of trust, commitment and loyalty – they have been untiring and unconditioned – the uncompromising strength of this, OUR family. They have remained by test and challenge steadfast.

Although many whose episodes have been mentioned in this book, there remains the need of notable mention of certain people most deserving that provided kindness and care when there was no calling of duty or relationship that bound them to act but did so in true and sincere friendship. Although each person named below has their own contribution in this journey, their episodes have not necessarily been exposed.

Prasad Bania
Malika Jagad
Mikki and Dilip Chabria
Gazanfar and Zarifa Rizvi
Ridas Žulys
Arūnas Krasauskas
Saulius Rudys
Saulius Juzukonis
Rolandas Kilmanas
Raimondas Petrėnas
Rimantas Baradinskas
Anthony Poullain
Joseph Seaman
Gaffree Party
Ričardas Kasparavičius
Bill Pahl
David Haahr
Lelon Caroll

Virgilijus Vasauskas
Ruslan Satikov
Justas Kapočius
Raimondas Žutautas
Doug Fanning
Philip Archer
W. Patrick Frost
Charles Somsakar
Photchanakarn Phanngarm
Carlo and Lorraine Ferrari
Labid Aziz
Nindy Singh
T. Raj Singh
Anna Ostakhova
Mike Pine
Kathleen Bachus
Mark Singh

Special Thanks to:

Juratė Sodeikienė: Her friendship, support, encouragement and home cooked meals gave comfort during the purgatory of over year in waiting for the Lithuanian decision.

Yana Leonova, whose friendship remains most valued and whose untiring efforts made this publication possible.

Mark Hirsch Esq., and Richard Rosenbaum Esq., respectively, my attorneys in the United States whose personal friendship and professionalism have gone above and beyond the call.

Howard Gressman
Kęstutis Skerbys
Jay Boccia
Minaz Aladdin
Prince Muzaffar Khan (Poncho)
Diego and Sonia Periea

Printed by

SPAUDA
Laisves ave. 60,
LT-05120, Vilnius
Lithuania